bad
lawyer

ALSO BY ANNA DORN

Vagablonde

A Memoir of Law and Disorder

bad lawyer

Anna Dorn

hachette
BOOKS

NEW YORK

Hachette Books
Hachette Book Group
1290 Avenue of the Americas
New York, NY 10104
HachetteBooks.com
Twitter.com/HachetteBooks
Instagram.com/HachetteBooks

First Edition: May 2021

Published by Hachette Books, an imprint of Perseus Books, LLC, a subsidiary of Hachette Book Group, Inc. The Hachette Books name and logo is a trademark of the Hachette Book Group.

The Hachette Speakers Bureau provides a wide range of authors for speaking events.

To find out more, go to www.hachettespeakersbureau.com or call (866) 376-6591.

The publisher is not responsible for websites (or their content) that are not owned by the publisher.

Print book interior design by Sean Ford.

Library of Congress Cataloging-in-Publication Data
Names: Dorn, Anna, author.
Title: Bad lawyer: a memoir of law & disorder / Anna Dorn.
Description: New York, NY: Hachette Book Group, Inc., 2021. | Includes bibliographical references.
Identifiers: LCCN 2020041710 | ISBN 9780306846526 (hardcover) | ISBN 9780306846557 (ebook)
Subjects: LCSH: Dorn, Anna. | Criminal defense lawyers—United States—Biography. | Practice of law—United States—Anecdotes. | Law—United States—Anecdotes. | Law schools—United States—Anecdotes.
Classification: LCC KF373.D597 A3 2021 | DDC 340.092 [B]—dc23
LC record available at https://lccn.loc.gov/2020041710

ISBNs: 978-0-306-84652-6 (hardcover), 978-0-306-84655-7 (ebook)

Printed in the United States of America

LSC-C

Printing 1, 2021

For Kitty

contents

contents

Introduction

The day I decided to write this book, I left a confidential legal document in a bar—and not just any bar but a German-style biergarten, where the servers wore traditional dirndls and lederhosen. Festive, perhaps, but not the best environment for a confidential document. Soon after I left, the barmaid came running after me, frantically waving my juvenile client's rap sheet in the golden afternoon light.

At the time, I was practicing indigent criminal appeals, meaning I got the case after my hopeless client had *already* lost at trial and my odds of achieving a favorable outcome were slight. But something about a disheveled, beribboned barmaid thrusting beer-stained files back into my hands after I'd had a few drinks made it all feel that much more fruitless.

I'd never really felt like a lawyer, but at this moment I felt particularly unqualified.

To be clear: Law school was never my dream. It was a profession pushed on me by my parents, teachers, *society* . . . whatever. It's not the worst thing that can happen to a person.

Law school was cushy, nowhere near as bad as people make it sound. It was definitely better than a job, and way easier than putting on a duvet cover.

At UC Berkeley, I wore leggings every day and played beer pong most nights, and my classmate who I later found out was American royalty (my lawyer has advised me to omit the family name) was always handing me Molly at parties. Honestly, the roughest thing about the experience was the idea that I'd someday have to *be* a lawyer. But then I'd turn on an episode of *Damages*, watch Glenn Close throw a stapler at someone's head, and think it looked kind of chic.

As it turned out, there was nothing sexy about being a lawyer. I had to wear a boxy suit and ingratiate myself to revolting old men who could never manage to keep their mouths closed while chewing a sandwich. I never saw the sunlight. Oh, and I was also very bad at it. Not because I wasn't smart enough, but more because I couldn't get myself to play by the rules—the draconian citation requirements, as if we don't all have Google; the slavish reverence for American tradition, as if our country doesn't have a vile past. When it comes down to it, the law is horny for rules in a way my rebellious ass could never get behind. And the legal system was so unjust. If I let myself care too much, I would probably end up in a mental hospital.

Mainly, I was trying to escape.

I spent most of my clerkship writing a novel in the body of a judicial order form and trying to convince the judges that no one should be punished for a misdemeanor. I mean, how could you possibly punish a homeless person for stealing a cup of soup?

In my stint as a criminal appellate attorney, I can't count how many times I filed the wrong document with the court by accident or mixed up client names in important emails. I've never shredded a document or read a contract all the way through. And, as my biergarten folly shows, I never took lawyer-client privilege or confidentiality ethics very seriously.

I wrote *Bad Lawyer* because I know that I'm not the only bad lawyer, and I'm definitely not the worst. I've seen prosecutors lie and file briefs so lazy their reasoning is "The defendant is guilty because he is not innocent."

Once, when I asked a friend for details about a recent case, she responded, "Top secret (I'll tell you later once I'm drinking)."

I've seen judges sipping on bourbon in chambers and perusing auctions on eBay instead of listening to homicide testimony.

I once watched a judge convict a defendant in a bench trial because he "couldn't tell what happened." So much for innocent until proven guilty.

When I first sat down to write this book, my Twitter feed was furious that a Supreme Court nominee—Kavanaugh—had sexually assaulted someone when he was seventeen. To me, a high-powered judge having sexually abused someone is not remotely surprising. I heard a woman on the radio call a judge "the highest arbiter of moral authority." Funny, I see judges as power-hungry narcissists, morally neutral at best.

When I lived in San Francisco's Bay Area, former Ninth Circuit judge Alex Kozinski was famous for his "movie nights," which my friend called "fun as long as you have a male chaperone"—otherwise, Kozinski would likely corner you into a weird conversation and stare idly at your breasts. (He's been accused of sexual misconduct by more than fifteen women, but denies all allegations, stating during his resignation that these women must have misunderstood his "broad sense of humor" and "candid way of speaking.")[1]

It's crazy the reverence the average American has for the Supreme Court, which legal historian Jacob Anbinder aptly calls "a reactionary conservative institution that has made like six good decisions in its 250 year existence."[2] All things considered, my former clients—alleged criminals—were more deserving of respect than most of the sitting members on the Supreme Court. At least they *wanted* to be good.

We may fetishize the law as a noble profession, but if my whack experiences in law school, courthouses, and law offices have taught me anything, it's that the law leaves much to be desired. *Bad Lawyer* isn't about just my own badness but also the badness of my peers, the badness of the system, and the badness of the law in general—namely, its inability to mediate disputes between people, which is what it was ostensibly designed to do.

It's the book no one wants to write—I don't particularly want to write it—but I feel like it needs to be said. Because law school is expensive as shit.

When I asked my lawyer friend to read over a draft of this book to make sure it doesn't contain anything "egregiously inaccurate," she responded:

"Anna, you know lawyers don't know shit about the law. It's our signature."

CHAPTER 1

The Parents

Whenever people asked about my dad while I was growing up, I'd quote Cher Horowitz in *Clueless*: "My dad's a litigator. That's the scariest type of lawyer."

The "law" was passed down in my family like a hideous heirloom. My dad was a lawyer. My grandfather was a lawyer. Most of my uncles are lawyers. And it wasn't just my family—most of the people I grew up with also had families full of lawyers. I was born and raised in what the *Washington Examiner* called "the lawyer capital of the world."[1]

One in twelve Washington, DC, residents is a lawyer (the national average is 1 in 260).[2] That meant most of my parents' friends and my friends' parents were lawyers. My dad's best friend has represented former president George H. W. Bush and former Penn State coach Joe Paterno. A friend's dad defended President Clinton against impeachment and was White House Counsel for Obama . . . and was later indicted for lying to federal prosecutors. Oh, and he is being represented by another one of my dad's friends.

You'll note something in common among all of these lawyers I've described: a Y chromosome.

Despite my two X chromosomes, the idea that I would someday become a lawyer always felt inevitable. I spoke early. I was good at school. The human body terrified me, still terrifies me, so being a doctor was out. I don't recall being interested in the law, but I was endeared to the idea of being right, of convincing someone else they were wrong, of intellectually embarrassing them. All throughout my childhood I watched my mother struggle to assert herself. I watched her get walked over and demeaned. I watched her shrink herself literally and figuratively. I watched how she'd abandon her own ambitions to do what was expected of her—to get married, raise a family, and accommodate that family's every whim. This could not be my fate. I needed to be somebody. I needed agency. Becoming a lawyer felt like a vehicle to respect. I also enjoyed the television show *The Practice*, and like most children of the nineties, I got most of my ideas of what adulthood should look like from television.

My dad was a good lawyer. He wasn't a good person, per se, but he was successful—a top international trade litigator. He was repeatedly recognized in the Washington, DC, Super Lawyers directory and *The Best Lawyers in America* and on some other lists. And, yes, we lived "inside the Beltway." He would frame these accolades and put them up around the house and then my mom would move them into the basement.

Though I often quoted *Clueless* to people who asked about my dad, my favorite movie was *Liar Liar*, a 1997 Jim Carrey film about a successful lawyer who frequently breaks promises to his son because he is focused on his work. The metaphor here is not subtle. When I was four going on five, I asked my mom whether she thought my dad would remember my birthday. She just shrugged. When I was twelve, I ran through a glass door and ended up in the emergency room. This was before cell phones, and when I couldn't reach my mom, I called my dad's office. He said he was in a meeting and hung up. In high school, bold friends asked if I even had a dad. (That was when the *Clueless* line came in handy.)

Cher was right; litigators are *scary*. My dad was scary. Scary when he was angry but even scarier when he wasn't.

When I was little, my dad told me that I was his favorite child. Shortly after, my sister said he said the same thing to her. My dad is seventy-two and has never served jury duty (as far as I know, he's ignored every single notice) and firmly does not believe in "objective truth."

Neither do I.

Another reason I liked *Liar Liar* was because it counteracted the stereotype that lawyers are somehow more rule-abiding than everyone else. In my experience, both as a kid and now as an adult, lawyers are even less principled than cops. A lawyer's job is literally to twist facts as far as they can possibly go in the client's favor. So why does everyone then act shocked and appalled when lawyers do bad things?

My dad's specialty was something called "antidumping," which I always thought was an unfortunate name. My crude understanding (thanks to a brief internship with his firm in high school) is that he fought against foreign businesses that illegally dropped their prices in the United States to unfairly compete with American businesses. He made it sound like noble work, but in retrospect I'm dubious, particularly because he was

3

defending American corporations, which, historically, have been anything but noble.

(My instinct is that the general public could benefit if foreign products were allowed to compete in the domestic market. More products, better prices—sounds good to me. I like Toblerone as much as the next bitch. But I don't know much about finance.)

While writing this book, my dad texted me that he was going to write a rebuttal to my book called Good Lawyer.

I responded, based on what?

My experience as a lawyer, he said.

Do you think your work made a positive contribution to society?

Yes, he responded. I saved hundreds of factories and tens of thousands of jobs in getting remedies against unfairly traded imports from China and other countries. I also provided jobs and successful career paths to many young lawyers. I feel really good about my legal career.

My dad worked at King & Spalding, which one Glassdoor reviewer referred to as a "firm full of sexist, racist partners."[3] The Atlanta-based firm is known for having Coca-Cola as a client and for being the defendant in a historic 1984 sex discrimination case, *Hishon v. King & Spalding*. The Supreme Court held that Elizabeth Hishon had the right to bring suit against the firm for denying her partnership bid on the basis of gender. That same year, at the company picnic some men at King & Spalding decided that it would be fun to stage a wet T-shirt contest starring the firm's female associates.[4] The men were less interested in breaking the company's glass ceiling than in watching women slip and slide all over it.

When I was twenty-seven and living in my childhood

bedroom, my dad invited me to dinner one day after work. I walked from the courthouse where I was clerking to the sushi restaurant in Foggy Bottom where my dad and I always ate out, which we typically did without my mom. (My parents aren't divorced, which is perplexing to me and anyone who has spent time in a room with them.) The restaurant was cold, sterile, and predictable—just like our relationship.

"Mom told me you, er . . . ," he stumbled.

I nervously sipped my Kirin Light, no idea where this was going. Normally, at these dinners, my dad talked about himself and then I talked about myself and neither of us listened to what the other person was saying.

"She told me you are dating someone," he continued.

I swallowed. "Yeah," I said. I was dating a woman for the first time, a fact I hadn't told either of my parents. I was firmly resisting the societal expectation that gay people must come out. It's an unfair burden to impose upon an already marginalized group.

I wasn't hiding anything from my dad, actively, but I wasn't going to start making announcements either. Announcements are tacky. Not my style. My parents ignored my dating life when I dated men and I expected them to ignore it when I dated women. This was the WASP way.

"You know," he said. I took another sip of my beer. I was terrified this was going to get cheesy. "King and Spalding was voted one of the best firms to work at for gays and lesbians."

I smiled, relieved. My dad's response was so misguided that I had to appreciate it. He'd responded to the news that I was a lesbian with a statistic, with *evidence*, as though it was moral support. It was so classic. Classic attorney, classic my father.

My dad *loved* being a lawyer. He'll say this even after—it seemed to me—King & Spalding pushed him out for being too old. His identity was so attached to being a lawyer that he had to hire a psychiatrist to prepare him for retirement, something he talked about for more than ten years before biting the bullet. To his credit, psychotherapy did make him easier to be around—he seemed, for the very first time, to actually listen when I spoke—but it couldn't fix the underlying problem, that my dad ultimately cared more about being respected within the Big Law hierarchy than anything else.

Once while I was in law school, my dad, mom, granny, and I were having drinks in our sunroom. My dad looked absent as we chitchatted about various relatives; his mind was elsewhere. As soon as he finished his Manhattan, he excused himself. "I have to go write this reply brief." He rubbed his hands together and grinned. I'd never seen him so excited. He was ready to destroy his opponent.

And in that moment, I felt very related to him. The excitement of leaving a social situation to get to the keyboard. Mind spinning with arguments that were begging to be sculpted into clean and logical paragraphs. For me, the only time life feels promising is when I'm about to put an idea to paper. It's the only time I feel confident and secure, like I know what's going to happen—and I'm in control. My dad relished that feeling, too.

Growing up, people always said my dad and I were similar—a comparison that deeply offended me. I guess we're both disciplined and self-absorbed, insecure and depressive. A law firm preys on these qualities and exploits them. Whereas I started psychoanalysis at eleven, my dad channeled his pathos into making money and generating status. He cherished his "top lawyer" accolades and bought gadgets he unsuccessfully used to woo his bratty children.

"Why did you want to be a lawyer?" I asked my dad when I was little.

"The richest person on my block was a lawyer," he said.

Touché. And yet.

Early on, I promised myself I would grow up to be nothing like him. I would fight my genetic conditioning and the frequent suggestions that I should become a successful lawyer like my father. I didn't care about money or status, I told myself. In high school, I became a Marxist. I stopped eating meat and buying clothes. I meditated to become less argumentative; my mantra was "tranquil." I wore hemp necklaces and spent most of my time in the darkroom, listening to Usher and getting a little high off photographic fixer, a mix of chemicals used in the final steps of processing film. Suddenly, flowers appeared magically on blank paper.

You know, typical white girl shit.

But fast-forward to when I was a junior in college, and it was time to start thinking about getting a job. I didn't want a job. I wanted to stay in school. I wanted to keep writing papers and reading books that had nothing to do with the practical realities of actual life. I didn't want to have to sell things, or myself, to the brainwashed masses. I was a Marxist!

"Anna, we should take an LSAT class," my friend Nate said one afternoon while we were buying Orbit gum in the student union during a break from class. We were seniors at the University of North Carolina at Chapel Hill. I chose that school because I didn't have the SAT scores for Yale—where culturally savvy brainiacs like Rory Gilmore went—and I did not want to go to a cliché liberal arts school in the Northeast like everyone else at my high school. At that time, the DC government would pay in-state tuition for DC residents at any state school in the country, so I decided to take advantage. My dream was UC Berkeley, but I was rejected. I got into UCLA and Michigan and UNC-Chapel Hill. UCLA was too far and Michigan was too cold, so UNC-Chapel Hill won out by default.

My dad had gone to UNC-Chapel Hill, and I was uncomfortable about so explicitly following in his footsteps.

"Why would we take an LSAT class?" I asked.

"For something to do," Nate said. "Our parents will be thrilled and won't make us get jobs and we can just stay in Chapel Hill over the summer and chill."

That sounded ideal. By this point, I preferred low-key Chapel Hill, with its lush, walkable streets and general lack of pretention, to stuffy, buttoned-up, pants-in-a-wad DC. Also, I was a little in love with Nate.

So we stayed in Chapel Hill for the summer and signed up for the Kaplan LSAT class, which took up only about six hours of our week. The rest of the time, we smoked weed and went on walks and frequented "grad student bars" and watched *Grey Gardens* over and over and over again. A near-perfect summer.

During one of our first practice tests, Nate stormed out of the room because the logic games frustrated him. He quit, so I was in the class alone. But I actually enjoyed studying for the exam, and even taking it. I liked how reducing the world to logic distracted my mind from the darker places it tended to go. Everything was theoretical, so in a way, nothing really mattered. It was less stressful than, say, figuring out my purpose in life, or thinking about the fact that one day I and everyone I know would die. Also, I wanted to get a good score. I had not yet fully meditated out my competitive side. How was I supposed to know I was smart without being validated by an institute of higher education?

My Floridian grandmother, whose husband (my grandfather) had gone to Harvard Law, wanted nothing more than to have a granddaughter in law school. She would even pay my tuition. This wasn't something she told me specifically; it was just something that was understood. (Luckily, due to her dementia, Granny still thinks I'm in law school. I graduated nearly ten years ago, but I'll take it.)

I would go to law school and it would be paid for. This was huge, because the exorbitant cost is the major obstacle to getting a law degree. You may go into law school wanting to save the planet, but debt forces you to eventually defend corporations accused of poisoning children.

But because I was going gratis, I could be a "good lawyer." The kind that advocates for vulnerable populations and defends people who are wrongly accused of crimes. Or at least, that's what I told myself. I didn't have to be like my dad.

I would change the world!

CHAPTER 2

The Internship

I decided to take a year off between college and law school to focus on my favorite hobby: smoking marijuana.

To this end, I moved to San Francisco, where the air smelled of cannabis and no one cared about Ivy League colleges. I'd always dreamed of living in California, the land of palm trees and mavericks, but I'd wanted to live in San Francisco specifically since my childhood obsession with *Full House*. In fact, the Olsen twins have been a guiding light for many of my life decisions.

I got an internship with the San Francisco Public Defender because my childhood best friend Amber—who was raised by public defenders—told me it would prepare me for law school. For those blessed to be unfamiliar, public defenders are government attorneys appointed to defend the indigent. In the 1960s, the Supreme Court held in *Gideon v. Wainwright* that the Sixth Amendment requires the state to provide a lawyer to defendants who can't afford one. It is challenging work with a noble goal.

My parents were confused by my decision. They wanted me

to get a paralegal job at a law firm. You know, the type of job that sets you up to make loads of money but that mostly involves photocopying and putting pieces of paper into binders. Amber's parents were more fun than mine. They threw crazy parties and said "fuck" and had good values. You know, like, they understood societal inequality and didn't think poor people "lacked discipline." I trusted their judgment. They weren't public defenders anymore, but they spoke about their early-career experiences at the DC Public Defender Service like it was college—wild and transformative and incredibly bonding.

Not long after I was accepted for the internship my senior year at UNC, I got a call from my mom's friend. I was on spring break in Florida.

"Anna," Linda said, "your mom is going to jail."

I laughed. I didn't believe her.

But then I remembered how flippant my mom could be toward the police. She got tons of speeding tickets, which she blamed on her bright red Volvo (for attracting attention), and she parked illegally all the time. As a kid, I thought the red-painted curb was where you were *supposed* to park. And whenever an officer confronted her, she would throw major attitude. Obviously, there were never any consequences. She was a frail WASP, basically invisible to the police.

Well, I guess after decades of this attitude, karma had caught up with her.

"What happened?" I asked, my voice quiet and measured.

My friends and I had stopped at my granny's house in Jacksonville on the way back to North Carolina, and at the moment she was driving us to lunch. Granny was yapping, and I didn't want to alarm her.

"We're at the dog park, and your mom was walking Jet and Georgia off-leash."

I tried not to laugh. Of *course* my mom would get arrested at the dog park. Was there a WASPier way to get arrested? Maybe on a horse.

"This awful park police officer came up and started writing a ticket, then grabbed your mom's wrist without warning. She tried to move her hand and he put her in handcuffs. Then she slipped out of the cuff to answer the phone, and he threw her on the ground! And then he put her in the cop car."

I was annoyed at my mom for giving the cop attitude, for trying to get out of handcuffs. I was also annoyed this had happened on my spring break, of all possible weeks. "So, what now?"

"We don't know," said Linda. "Caroline and I have the dogs. We can't get a hold of your father." Of course. "We've called Bill and Wesley." Both of my mom's friends were married to— you guessed it—lawyers.

"Okay," I said. "Is there anything I can do?"

"Not at the moment," Linda said. "We just wanted to let you know."

After we hung up, Granny asked if everything was okay. I lied and said it was.

Well, it wasn't okay. It wasn't totally okay, at least. My mom was booked on a Friday afternoon. She went to DC Central Cell, an urban jail known for its "inhumane conditions."[1] Linda called me later that evening to tell me my mom would be there at least overnight, and they still couldn't reach my dad. Bill and Wesley were working on it. My mom's friend Judy called her friend Ethel Kennedy, RFK's widow, who said she would call Greg Craig, who had been appointed Barack Obama's White House Counsel.

I didn't know what to say or think or feel. This whole thing was insane. My fifty-eight-year-old, 120-pound mom was in DC jail for what started as a dog-off-leash offense. And White House Counsel had been notified. And my dad, a lawyer, was nowhere to be found. (Again, the fact that my parents remain married is bewildering.) And I was in Florida, with my grandmother, afraid she would find out and have a heart attack and it would all be my fault. It would've been a classic setup for a sitcom episode if it wasn't my *actual life*.

My mom was in jail for two nights. She didn't eat anything the entire time. She shared a cell with a crack addict named G. At the arraignment, she took a plea deal and ended up with community service. Her lawyer wanted to try the case because he thought she was likely to win, but a trial would be expensive and time-consuming and my mom didn't mind doing community service, which she coincidentally served at an after-school care center called MOMMIES.

On the bright side, when my mom got out, she was suddenly thrilled that I was going to be a public defender.

———

I really had no idea what to expect at the internship in San Francisco and didn't do much research beforehand. To be honest, I was mostly just excited to be living in a city where weed was legal.

I moved in with a couple I met on Craigslist, mainly because their ad said "420 encouraged"—an enthusiastic leap from the standard "420 friendly." Their apartment was on the top floor of a classic Victorian; from the balcony, you could see the bay sparkle turquoise in the distance. It was also in an ideal location. I could walk to both the 24th Street Mission BART hub and all the bars designed for twentysomething stoners who wanted to shout along to "California Love" while staring vacantly at neon lights. I could walk to all the famous taco spots and a thousand Indian restaurants. I could walk to Noe Valley, which kind of looked like a New England fishing village and had a Whole Foods and lots of farm-to-table restaurants. And then of course there was Dolores Park, which sat on a hill and had an untarnished view of the city—when it wasn't completely shrouded in coastal fog or clouds of medical-grade Indo.

My roommates were older, vestiges of the pre-Google Mission that no longer exists—underemployed lapsed punks who drew cartoons in their spare time. All of their friends were artists, drug addicts, and/or petty criminals. On a good day, this all felt very exciting; when I was going through a bad high, a bit less so.

One time, I woke up in the middle of the night to their friend Austin banging on the front door. I let him in and he promptly passed out on the couch. The next morning, my roommate Hannah scolded me. "Do *not* let Austin in late at night again," she warned.

"I thought he was your friend," I said, confused.

"He is," she replied. "But he's sketchy. He's stolen from us before."

I was kind of alarmed that my roommates' best friend was

a verified thief. But it also made me feel, you know, alive. *Recklessly alive.*

Another time, I came home in the middle of the day and Hannah immediately started petting my hair. She wasn't the most affectionate, so this shocked me at first—until she told me she was "candy flipping," which is when you take acid and Molly at the same time. I told her I had never taken either drug and she giggled and said I was "adorable."

Soon after, a tiny white girl named Clover walked in and announced, "Fucking pigs, man." She had jet-black hair and wore feather earrings and probably weighed ninety pounds. I quickly learned that she had come to the apartment straight from jail, where she'd been locked up for a graffiti charge. She had been in jail numerous times, was raised by wealthy LA attorneys, and subsisted primarily on Jack Daniels. She was the prototype of an overprivileged delinquent, and I felt like I was looking in a funhouse mirror.

Afterward, I started noticing her "Clover" tags all over the neighborhood. They haunted me a little bit.

My first day at work, the intern coordinator said, "Criminal law isn't rocket science." The hard part, she said, is that I'd be working on cases that included very grisly facts. She put me in domestic violence court in the mornings and in the research department in the afternoons. The research department sounded much more appealing. I could sit at a computer and look shit up all day.

Domestic violence court was, unsurprisingly, very depressing.

My supervisor was a paralegal who was going through a divorce, and he made me show up early to wheel in the case files on a big rolling cart so he could sleep in.

As it turned out, most court matters were about coordinating schedules. I never saw an actual trial in domestic violence court. I just kept showing up and they kept moving dates around. The judge was always scolding me for being on my phone, which at that point had a neon-pink cover—not exactly discreet. But I didn't care; it was my first iPhone and I was really, really in love. I was mostly scrolling Instagram, which had just come out that year, and I was an early adopter—anything to pluck me from the intolerable discomfort of the present moment.

When I did put down my phone, my interactions left much to be desired. I got hit on almost every day in domestic violence court. I was never scared, just mostly confused that the defendants—who were required to be there, while the lawyers and judges moved dates around—would choose that particular venue to pick up a date. I guess Tinder hadn't really taken off yet, so who am I to judge? Sometimes I was even flattered. One defendant in particular developed an intense obsession with me. He would bring me cheap gifts from Chinatown—paper lanterns and jade trinkets. I never told anyone at the office about it. And it wasn't until years later, in a law school seminar on "boundaries," that I learned it was completely unethical of me to have accepted the gifts.

In the research department, I was paired with a charismatic lunatic named Fernando. He often bragged that he had once thrown a copy of the California Penal Code at an intern's head. On my first day, he took me to an expensive lunch with his other intern, Chris, who was studying criminal justice at SF City College.

At lunch, Fernando announced he was on a diet. He explained to the server how he wanted his salmon prepared as though he was arguing to a panel of appellate judges. *No* butter. *No* oil. *No* potatoes. *Nothing* but the meat itself, lightly cooked. Literally just the fish. When the salmon arrived, he took out a miniature scale and weighed it.

Fernando didn't look like someone who was neurotic about nutrition. He was relatively fit but hefty. In the gay world, he would likely classify as a bear—but clean-shaven. He had spiky black hair, a style that I assume was popular in the early nineties, and alert brown eyes.

Once Fernando asked me to get him a chicken burrito from the food truck outside the office. When I got to the stand, the cashier asked me if I wanted a small or large. Fernando was on a diet, so I said small.

When I returned with the burrito, Fernando wasn't in his office, so I left it on his desk. Half an hour later, he emerged from his office holding the burrito, a livid expression on his face.

"Anna, what the fuck is this?"

"A chicken burrito," I said. "Like you asked."

"Why is it so small?" He squinted at me.

"I got you the small," I said. "I figured that's what you would want."

"I said *large!*" he screamed.

"You just said chicken burrito," I said. "You're on a diet, so I figured you would want the small."

He got up in my face. "Anna," he said. "I said *large*. I have it written in my food journal. I have to consume the *exact* number of calories every meal that are accounted for in my food journal, otherwise my diet is ruined. Now the entire day is *fucked*!" He walked away and slammed the burrito in the trash.

Theatrics aside, Fernando's behavior was fairly innocent compared to that of most attorneys there. At our Christmas party, the box with the cash donations for the office disappeared.

I was outside with the French office manager when the news of the missing donation box started circulating.

"I didn't know you smoked," Victor said to me. I didn't really know him, and I didn't really smoke. I just wanted an excuse to stand outside and get away from the crowd.

"I don't," I said. I inhaled hard.

"You must feel dizzy then," Victor said.

"I do," I said, leaning against the building. Our office party was in a shady bar in SoMa, which is mostly start-ups now but back then was teeming with crackheads and prostitutes.

"Valencia took the donation box," a woman said, suddenly approaching our cigarette circle. I didn't recognize this woman, but I did know of Valencia. She was one of the top felony attorneys in the office.

"Why?" I asked.

The woman shrugged. "She's a drunk." She bummed a cigarette from Victor. "She always does these sorts of things."

———

Fernando talked more about his diets that year than almost anything else, except maybe Woody Allen movies or his steadfast belief that lesbians were domestic terrorists. I was uncertain about my sexuality at the time, which added a weird layer to the whole lesbian obsession.

The research department attorneys (like Fernando) didn't typically go to court, but whenever a big murder was closing, the whole office would go to watch. And so we sat in.

"Latte thief," Fernando once muttered while eyeing the butch prosecutor storm into the courtroom.

I don't remember the facts of the case. By this point, all the rapes and murders were blending together. It sounds callous to put it that way, but becoming detached was the only way to survive. Otherwise, lawyers developed drinking problems or became violent themselves. It was a dark place, the Hall of Justice, but Fernando made me feel safe, or maybe he just distracted me from all the madness. He certainly kept me entertained. He was my first real friend in California.

I do remember the attorney we were there to watch. All the homicide attorneys in our office were hot and this one was the hottest. His trial name—yes, like a stage name—was River Fox, and he allegedly fucked all the interns and rode a motorcycle blackout drunk every night. Like James Dean, but with a briefcase. (Actually, he probably carried his files in a backpack. Most public defenders did.)

"Excuse me?" I asked.

"Oh," Fernando whispered. "I haven't told you about the latte thieves. They run this town—especially the Hall of Justice."

"Huh?"

"Shh," he snapped; the judge was giving us a look.

Stomping around in her boots (San Francisco Superior Court was very lax when it came to courtroom attire; this was San Francisco, after all), the prosecutor claimed the community would be in danger unless the accused was charged with the most serious count on the indictment. Standard prosecutorial closing.

Honestly, all closings were the same. The defense would stress the presumption of innocence and the legal standard of proof beyond a reasonable doubt, arguing that the prosecution failed to reach that very high standard. The prosecution would stress the severity of the crime and the importance of retribution, deterrence, and keeping the public safe. (The San Francisco district attorney then was Kamala Harris. Ten years later, she ran for president and she did not get my vote—I continue to see her as the opposition.)

After the closing argument, of which I have no specific memory other than it was delivered by James Dean with a backpack, Fernando and I walked back to the office against strong wind gusting off the bay. On the way, Fernando revealed the origin story for the hyperspecific lesbian nickname he had just used for the butch prosecutor on the other side of the case.

"So a few years ago," Fernando told me, "this lesbian in a 'Dykes for Hillary' T-shirt stole my latte at Peet's Coffee. It was very clearly *my* latte." He was becoming red in the face, indignant. Suddenly, his expression shifted to a playful grin. "I know a few women in the office who've stolen a latte . . . mostly in college . . . if you get my drift."

Then my face turned red.

———

Fernando took me out to a lot of fancy meals that year. As a single, childless fortysomething who'd received a major payout on a recent lawsuit (he never told me the details), he was drowning in cash. He took taxis to work every day (this was pre-Uber) and often bought expensive French pastries for the office, which he never ate because he was always on a diet.

At one of our lunches, I confided in Fernando that I, too, had "stolen a latte or two."

I'd slept with a lot of men (what, like it's hard?), but I was also fresh off a summer fling with a woman. I was living in DC with my parents, awaiting the West Coast move and teaching tennis at a computer camp (the kids were about as enthusiastic about tennis as you'd expect). Like any emotionally stunted brat, I threw parties at my parents' house well into my twenties. At the summer kickoff, I had invited Emma, an out bisexual I knew from college. She ended up being one of the last remaining guests. Dripping wet from the pool, I told her I was going to bed and she could sleep over if she wanted. This was not intended to be flirtatious, but more a polite gesture. At least that's what I told myself.

I went up to my room and immediately threw up in the toilet. A total aphrodisiac. After I brushed my teeth and climbed into bed, Emma pounced on me. I'd made out with women before, but this was the first time my lesbian behavior wasn't art-directed by lurky bros at a party. It was the first time I felt like a woman actually wanted me.

And I loved it.

"Have you done this before?" she asked.

"Of course," I lied.

It was easy, though. I have a vagina, so I know what feels good. Emma was very beautiful and theatrical when she came, a welcome relief from the revolting performance that is the male orgasm.

Emma texted me a week later when I was at my camp-counselor orientation to invite me to an underground rap show. It was all very exciting, escaping my tragic suburban summer job to make out with a bisexual in a steamy dive-bar bathroom.

Later that summer, at some basement dance party, this dorky man was all over Emma. I found it funny, the way he was trying so hard, completely oblivious to our flirtation. "Who is that?" I had finally asked.

"Oh," she had said. "He's nobody." (They're currently married.)

When I told Fernando an edited version of this story, he assumed an empathetic expression and told me my secret was safe with him.

But back in the office that afternoon, Fernando announced, "Anna told me she stole a latte!" to a random group congregated in the hall.

Fernando was often shitty to me that summer, like when he made me write his briefs while he watched *Deconstructing Harry* in his office, or the multiple times when he told me I needed to wear more makeup, or when he'd publicly proclaim in professional settings that I was a lesbian. He was my first legal boss, and he gave me a strong message that it wasn't okay to be who I was. But I could never be mad at him because he took care of me, and isn't a roast the highest form of flattery? My relationship with Fernando reminded me of my relationship with the law in general. They were both adversarial and abrasive and told me I was wrong for being myself, but I was endeared to them nonetheless. Sass is my first language, and I like to be kept on my toes.

I guess I also like to be punished.

About a month after Fernando broadcast my big secret, I got a boyfriend, Kei—an old friend from high school. When we were both home for Christmas, our friendship turned romantic. He lived in London, which I found very glamorous, and was getting his master of fine arts at The Slade, which all the Young British Artists had attended, which I also found very glamorous. There was an eight-hour time difference between London and San Francisco, so he would wake up in the middle of the night to talk on the phone when it was convenient *to me*. He would also visit me all the time, as he was twenty-four and still had access to his father's Amex. We would get high and walk around San Francisco and take pictures of each other with the DSLR I'd stolen from my dad. He was also very femme; he had gorgeous long black hair I was often jealous of and wore designer jeans he'd jacked from his sister. When we walked into restaurants, the hostess would say "right this way, ladies," and that always felt nice.

So, with my femme boyfriend halfway across the world and most of my friends on the East Coast, I was beyond grateful for Fernando—even if he was kind of an asshole. He was rude to my face in a way that felt safe and familiar and frankly very East Coast. My favorite memories are when he took me to see *Precious* at the historic Balboa Theatre and we both cried, and when he let me write an entire appellate brief that we ended up winning.

In that case, the defendant was convicted of a DUI after being arrested at a checkpoint. Before trial, he had filed a motion to suppress, arguing that the checkpoint was unconstitutional, which the lower court had denied. In the case that set the governing precedent, *Ingersoll v. Palmer*, the California

Supreme Court held that DUI checkpoints are constitutionally permissible as long as certain standards are met to "minimize the intrusion on motorists" and protect their Fourth Amendment rights.

On appeal, we reargued that the checkpoint at issue did not meet these standards, which include factors like whether drivers are stopped according to a neutral formula, whether the length of the checkpoint reflects "good judgment" on the part of law enforcement, and whether the average length and nature of the detention are minimized.

If these factors seem vague, please know that all legal standards are purposely vague to account for the variety of factual situations that can arise. If this seems dry, please know that criminal law is by far the most interesting area of the law. You can see why so many lawyers turn to drugs and alcohol.

But now we get to the fun part—taking advantage of the vagueness and using salty rhetoric to convince a court that you are right!

We argued that five of the six *Ingersoll* factors were not met in our case. The appellate court agreed that the government failed to sustain its burden on four of the *Ingersoll* factors. (According to the Constitution, it is always the government's burden to prove the defendant's guilt beyond a reasonable doubt. The defendant is presumed innocent, meaning the defendant has no obligation to prove anything. But, obviously, that's not how it works in practice.) Anyway, the court reversed the denial of the motion to suppress.

We won!

And I got my first hit. This druggy feeling, the high of the California government, the institution I was being paid to fight against, validating my efforts, telling me I was right. I won. I beat the odds. I defended a criminal against the state and I won.

It was the best drug I'd ever tried.

Okay, fine, maybe the second best. Maybe third. Top five for sure.

CHAPTER 3

Acceptance

I was learning a lot from Fernando, I guess, but my internship was unpaid, so I got a nanny job for cash. Before my interview, I asked my boyfriend for advice. He said, "Don't be yourself," I guess because I don't project a very maternal vibe. I'm a thinker, not a nurturer. But the kid's parents were pretentious, and they liked that I was going to law school. I got the job taking care of their little baby, who was just eighteen months old. Her parents instructed me to read her *The Economist* every day, which I of course did not do even one day. I let her watch TV, which was strictly forbidden, because it seemed to make her happy.

Maybe I was more nurturing than I realized.

One day I went to work at my internship and Fernando looked like he'd seen a ghost. I thought a family member had died. He'd already lost two brothers when he was younger, and I couldn't handle him losing another. His life was tragic enough. I was scared to ask what was wrong, and luckily I didn't have to.

"Anna," he whisper-yelled. "Get in here."

I nervously approached his office and, once inside, he quickly closed the door behind me. "I've been sanctioned by the Court of Appeal." He continued to speak in a hushed tone.

I swallowed. A part of me was relieved. No one was dead.

"They say I misrepresented the law." His eyes were wide with worry. He'd cited a case as supporting his argument when it actually held the opposite view. I don't remember the facts of the appeal Fernando was sanctioned for, or even what the charge was, but the error was something along the lines of Fernando claiming that "*Ingersoll v. Palmer* holds DUI checkpoints are constitutionally permissible under all circumstances." As I explained in the previous chapter, that statement is not correct. (I do not blame you at all if you zoned out on the legal speak.) Put simply: he said a case said something it didn't say.

I was shocked. Fernando was typically so meticulous. He was a Capricorn! But I was also afraid. I didn't know what would happen to him, whether he would be disbarred or what. Fernando's job was his everything. Even though he often seemed to hate it, he didn't appear to have much else going on in his life. I never heard him talk about boyfriends or going on dates. When he talked about his friends, they were mostly people from the office. "The office" made an appearance in nearly all of his sentences.

The situation was especially unfair given that the government misrepresented cases and facts all the time.

Also, the case Fernando misrepresented wasn't a major case on which the appeal hinged. It was just a minor point cited in his reply brief. It didn't really seem like a big deal to me. But we were representing criminals, which meant it was always an uphill battle, and the courts would take any opportunity to make things difficult for us. The official legal standard is *innocent until proven guilty*, but that was not how it really worked. Once a person was charged with a heinous crime, everyone involved saw them differently, including judges and juries. It's human nature to judge the person accused of violence and want to avenge the victim. (And that is always prosecutors' stated goal, although in practice they never really seemed to take victims' or society's interests to heart—to me it looked like they just wanted to punish people.)

Beyond that, our clients were mostly poor people of color, and we all know how implicit bias works. Criminal defense attorneys have all the odds stacked against us. There is no room for error.

In a subsequent petition addressing the error, Fernando explained to the court that he wrote the brief at a time when his mom was very sick and he was preoccupied but that his mistake was innocent.

Finally, at a hearing where Fernando was interrogated by the entire panel—the court removed the sanctions.

Years later, when I practiced indigent criminal appeals on my own, I realized how easy it was to piss off the court, and the hoops they make you jump through when you make a mistake. I was never sanctioned, but I was always afraid I would be after seeing how close Fernando had gotten to being on the other side of justice. I was always nervous about getting scolded or slapped with a malpractice suit for a minor typo. But I was even more worried about my clients. I always felt way too careless to have their liberty in my hands. That never changed.

Nonetheless, I still applied to law school, the goal being to get into one of the top schools, because at that point I wasn't sure how else I would feel worthy or purposeful without the validation of an elite institution of higher learning. I applied to the best schools in California, which I found with a simple Google search in between buying burritos for Fernando and pointedly not reading *The Economist* to the baby. When I wasn't on the clock, I was applying to law schools or getting faded in public parks.

I smoked weed every single day—back then, far before every bitch in Lululemon carried around a CBD pen. In 2009, stoners were still sort of associated with hippies. Slackers. Degenerates. Dirty people who listened to *jam bands*. I resented this; the music element of this stereotype was the most offensive to me. God forbid someone were to associate me with *Phish*. I loved rap music, hip-hop, R & B. Something would happen to me when the cannabis tickled my throat; I'd immediately start scrolling my iTunes, and I'd crank the volume all the way up, hoping that a confident voice spitting over throbbing bass could drown out all my self-doubt.

Cannabis put me in touch with a lot of hip-hop I'd been too young (and perhaps too sober) to appreciate before. *Aquemini. Reasonable Doubt. Illmatic. All Eyez on Me.* And most important: *Ready to Die.*

I became *obsessed* with Biggie Smalls. It's so embarrassing, looking back on it. I bought a blacklight Biggie poster for my room. I was *that* white girl. Insufferable! But Christopher Wallace was just such a poet to me! And I hate poetry! But the way his voice rode the beat, it was like magic. And it was all so heavy. I would walk around the Mission in my Ann Taylor Loft dress, blasting "Suicidal Thoughts" in my headphones: *When I die, fuck it, I wanna go to hell / 'Cause I'm a piece of shit, it ain't hard to fucking tell.*

My enthusiasm for cannabis, it turned out, went hand in hand with my work in criminal defense. I didn't realize it then, but all of these albums brimmed with references to the criminal justice system. Jay-Z's best album, an album I didn't really discover until thirteen years after its release in 1996, was named after the standard of proof used in criminal cases, the one lawyers discussed in court, the one I wrote about every single day at work: *reasonable doubt.*

And then, of course, there was "99 Problems," from the *Black Album*, an album I'd learned to drive to that is steeped in criminal defense lingo: *Well, my glove compartment is locked, so is the trunk and the back / And I know my rights so you gon' need a warrant for that.* The introduction to a rather famous law review article begins: "I'm writing about ["99 Problems"] now because it's time we added it to the canon of criminal pedagogy."[1]

Amen. The reason a lot of marginalized groups end up in jail, beyond being unfairly targeted by police officers, is because they don't know their rights during illegal searches. Jay-Z explained these rights, in a straightforward manner, in a catchy pop song. It was activism at its least annoying.

There was also Biggie's "Hypnotize," where Biggie raps about kidnapping the prosecutor's daughter in order to convince him to throw the case, a truly terrifying premise. But I was obsessed with the line: *Let's face it, not guilty, that's how I stay filthy.* For some tacky reason, I thought it would make a great tagline if I ever started a criminal defense practice. (My reasoning being: I would get filthy rich off all my not-guilty verdicts, all while keeping shitty cops accountable.)

30

When people asked me why I wanted to do criminal defense, I would say, without irony, "Because it's where the badasses are." And, at twenty-three, I was starting to feel like one. I was smoking weed every day. Living with criminals. Defending criminals. Receiving gifts from people who beat their wives and writing memos on behalf of alleged rapists. It was a far cry from the white-shoe law firm where my dad had spent his entire adult life.

I just wanted to be cool. I didn't think about how inappropriate and problematic it was that I, a blonde woman and descendant of at least one US president (don't get too excited; according to my granny, it was Polk, and I hardly know who that is), was getting a strange high off my proximity to poverty and crime.

But at least I was on the "good side." I was helping people who lacked the resources to advocate for themselves, whose rights had been trampled upon by the police and generations of systemic racism and injustice. That was the refrain at the San Francisco Public Defender, at all public defender offices. We were good, noble, and the prosecutors were bad, evil. Honestly, it's about as morally nuanced as *Harry Potter*.

———

I'd literally just hit a bong when they called, so the call felt extra special. The voice on the phone said that I'd been accepted to UCLA Law. My college friend Henry was visiting, which was perfect for celebration purposes. After I called in sick for the next day at my internship, Henry and I split an Adderall and let loose. We went to Beauty Bar, a nightclub decorated like a retro salon. My last memory of that evening was Henry dipping me and dropping me on the floor.

"We were a hit last night," I told Henry in the morning.

"I don't know, Anna," he said. "I think we offended a lot of people."

I wasn't entirely sure what he was talking about. This was how a lot of my twenties went. I would be drinking and having fun and then I would be horizontal, and in the morning I wouldn't remember much of what occurred.

UCLA acceptance was nice, but it was not enough.

I actually had also gotten into University of Virginia Law, where my dad went and where I absolutely did not want to go. But I considered UCLA the first law school I was accepted into because there was no legacy connection. UVA was officially out. I went to the South for college and I was not going back.

And UCLA had even called me on the phone, which made me feel momentarily important.

But I wanted to go to Stanford or Berkeley, the two best law schools in California. It's said that where you go to law school matters for your legal career. The better the school, the better the career prospects. But I didn't care about career prospects. I just wanted a prestigious institution of higher education to validate me.

I'd gone to a state school for undergrad and that made me feel insecure about my intelligence, and about every other aspect of my being. I'd always gotten good grades, but anyone could get good grades, especially at UNC-Chapel Hill. I needed to get into a top law school so I would know I was worthy. It wasn't rational. It was neurotic. And law school is kryptonite for neurotics.

Then, an acceptance letter to USC arrived. I immediately threw it on the floor and proceeded to have sex with Kei. At the time, my art school boyfriend was starting to make me question whether I wanted to be a lawyer at all. I was regularly attending art shows, getting into conceptual artists like Felix Gonzalez-Torres, and reading critical theory by Susan Sontag and Gilles Deleuze. Kei was always trying to convince me I was an artist, which I always thought I was, but I was too attached to standard metrics of achievement to really embrace the idea.

Not long after my USC acceptance, I was rejected by Stanford.

Things weren't looking good for me. I was starting to feel like a total moron. I didn't even tell my parents about USC. It was too embarrassing. I had to go to Berkeley. There would be no other way.

Around that time, Georgetown Law called me on the phone and told me they wanted to schedule an alumni interview. Georgetown Law is considered a good school. It's even some people's dream school. It's also in DC, the city I grew up in. I should have been even a little excited about it.

I wasn't.

I hated DC, and Georgetown wasn't Stanford. But I figured it wouldn't hurt to interview. So I put on my best moccasins and took the BART to the Financial District, where I met with a sorority-looking young associate—shiny hair, bauble necklace, uptalk for days—in a fancy office made of glass.

"Don't you just *miss* DC?" She beamed. Apparently, she had grown up there, too, and had gone to one of my rival high schools. Why she missed it was beyond me. San Francisco was one of the prettiest cities in the world and no one tried to talk to you about their congressional internship.

"No," I said. "Not at all."

Then I realized, oops, she probably wanted me to say yes since that's where Georgetown is. At the end of the interview, she said she could tell I "didn't really want to go to Georgetown."

I backtracked and said, "I'd *love the opportunity to attend such a reputable institution.*" The sorority girl could smell my BS.

A few days later, I got a letter informing me I had been waitlisted at Georgetown.

Soon after, I got a letter from Berkeley.

The envelope was fucking thin: I was crushed.

I was waitlisted.

I immediately texted Amber, who was also applying to law school and knew much more about the process than I did. Amber was always my go-to bitch when it came to law-related things. We had been friends since fourth grade and were obsessed with *Legally Blonde.* We saw ourselves in Elle and Vivian. Amber was Vivian, the cunty brunette achiever. And I was Elle, the vapid blonde who's smarter than she looks. Amber was the type who went to informational sessions and researched the law school application process. I was always too self-indulgent and spacey to be bothered with such mundane, practical tasks.

You have to write a letter of continued intent, she texted me back instantly.

Huh?

Write them a letter detailing your experiences at the public defender office and expressing that you will absolutely go to Berkeley if you get in, she said. Get Fernando to write something too. That way they'll know you're serious.

Right away, I told Fernando, who was excited to do a project unrelated to the law. I sent my letter to Berkeley at the end of the week and hoped for the best.

———————

When my internship ended in May, I returned to DC for the summer. I'd heard nothing from Berkeley, so I enrolled at UCLA. I spent a month in Europe with Kei. He lived in London, and we figured after six months of him flying halfway around the world to see me, I should probably visit him. I'd studied abroad in London in college but this time enjoyed seeing a new side of it, an artsier side that felt more local and less touristy. One weekend we took the Chunnel to Paris, something I'd always wanted to do, even though the idea of being underwater for that long terrified me. I survived the Chunnel, but our relationship did not. We broke up in Paris, in the Hotel Amour—which was 100 percent worth it for the irony alone.

I returned to DC a little earlier than expected, and it was nice to have some time to relax before law school. My parents didn't love that I was going to UCLA, not that they really loved any of my life decisions. UCLA and UVA were pretty equally ranked at the time, but not in their minds. My parents didn't know anyone who had gone to UCLA Law, which to them suggested it was not good.

One afternoon while scrolling Tumblr in my childhood bedroom, I noticed an email from Berkeley. I'd been admitted off the waitlist!

I quickly canceled my enrollment at UCLA and flew to Berkeley to find an apartment. I signed a lease on a dingy little studio near campus. It had a haunted energy and was perpetually filled with the sounds of undergraduates partying. And I loved it.

On the plane ride back to DC, I dreamed about telling people I was going to Berkeley Law. Berkeley. Berkeley! I had bought a Berkeley tank top and bumper sticker, and when I got home, I proudly stuck my Berkeley bumper sticker on the back of my Saab. And then I filled up my car and drove to the West Coast.

CHAPTER 4

Law School

The first day of law school, I wore a suit. A black one with a striped blue button-down blouse. I thought this was what I was supposed to wear. I guess I wanted to look professional, which in retrospect, wasn't that hard to do—considering the first classmates I spoke to were drunk.

"Do you know where we're supposed to go?" I asked the first guy I saw.

"It seems like we're supposed to... *thataway*," he said. He pointed sloppily at some people approaching a big, daunting door.

"Sorry," another guy said. "We pregamed a bit."

They were both wearing T-shirts and jeans.

"I'm Mike," said the first guy.

"Trey," said the second.

"I got in off the waitlist," I blurted. This quickly became a tic. I needed everyone to know I was let in as a last resort, Berkeley's last-ditch effort to fill the class.

"I got off the waitlist, too," Mike said.

I didn't know it yet, but a lot of my first law school friends would be straight men. Cut to today: I do not have a single straight male friend. I don't care about sports or the stock market or their dicks. But as I looked around my new classroom, I recognized the type of off-putting female achievers I grew up with in DC. I wanted nothing to do with them. They had that spookily put-together and hyperalert expression. Generally, the type of woman who scares the shit out of me. Their hair was shiny and straight and freshly trimmed. Their voices were polite and pageant-like, but with an underlying tinge of aggression. They were on Earth to play some sort of weird game. When they spoke to you, they seemed to want to know one thing: *Can you help me win?*

I couldn't help anyone win. I didn't even have a basic knowledge of the legal system when I started law school, even after my internship. I didn't know the difference between a trial court and an appellate court, or state and federal court. And I didn't expect the weird vocabulary that came with law school, which felt unnecessarily elitist.

At orientation, we learned law students would be organized into three main modules, or, colloquially, "mods," each containing around ninety students. We took all of our large, lecture-style classes—Torts, Criminal Law, Property, Contracts—with our mod.

We were also broken down into "small mods," groups of around thirty, with whom we took all of our large classes in addition to small classes like Civil Procedure and Legal Research and Writing. Mods sort of dictated the social organization of the class; I remained friends with classmates from my small mod for most of law school. I was in "Mod 2," my small mod, which was led by Professor Hopson, who taught Civil Procedure. Neither of the drunk boys were in my small mod, but Mike was in my larger mod.

After the welcome talk for all students, Mod 2 convened in the classroom with Hopson, who was an older professor with a sweet, grandfatherly vibe. He'd coddle us like we were babies as opposed to law students except he never remembered our names and kept cold beer in his office. Typically, "Civ Pro" is a tough class—a complicated body of procedural rules civil courts used to adjudicate lawsuits—but "Hoppy" was so nice that he made it easy for us.

My drunk friends told me school doesn't matter much until the end of the semester, toward exam time, and I took that information to heart. I spent most of my first few weeks hiking around Berkeley's Tilden Park and meeting friends for drinks in San Francisco. I went to class and did the reading, of course, but that wasn't particularly time-consuming.

I loved going into the city and telling my friends, most of whom worked dead-end jobs, as we were twenty-three years old, that I was a student at Berkeley Law.

———

Some weeks later Professor Hopson invited the small mod over for a barbecue at his stately house in Piedmont, a fancy neighborhood on the border of Berkeley and Oakland. He also invited our Criminal Law professor, Nicole Porter.

Suddenly, I found myself in a small group surrounding Professor Porter. Most of the students seemed to love her. But I was dubious. She was friendly in that pageant-like, borderline-hostile way that I find creepy. She had clerked for Sotomayor and mentioned this during every single class. To be fair, clerking for a Supreme Court justice is a *big deal*. It's probably the hardest legal job to land, save actually being a Supreme Court justice, and it opens pretty much every door you want afterward.

Although I didn't know this at the time. But after being surrounded by law students for three years, I couldn't help but learn about clerkships and how they were fetishized. Essentially, judges are busy, and law clerks are recent law graduates who do a lot of their work for them. Many judicial opinions are authored by their law clerks. I recall a classmate telling me she slept with a Ninth Circuit law clerk the way a Los Angeles lesbian would brag about banging Kristen Stewart.

I watched my classmates salivate when Professor Porter mentioned clerking for Sotomayor. And it was obvious that they, like her, were on Earth to play the game: suck up to the right people and maybe get recruited to teach at Stanford or Harvard or Yale. All the students at Berkeley seemed to want to go to Stanford or Harvard or Yale, and all the teachers at Berkeley wanted to teach at Stanford or Harvard or Yale. No one really seemed to want to be at Berkeley Law except me.

That made me more of a spectator. A voyeur, really. At least that's the way I liked to think of myself. But as I stood among the crowd of little high achievers, caped in my Ann Taylor Loft striped blouse and ripped jean shorts, I felt torn between the need to feel worthy of this historical male institution, Berkeley or law in general, and its members—or just to give it a big middle finger. I'd seen these sort of gender relations play out since birth growing up with my mom and dad. But Professor Porter was the shining, shimmering, do-no-wrong matriarch that the other female students seemed to aspire to become. To me, Professor Porter was gross, a pawn in a patriarchy that gave women a very narrow space to occupy in professional settings. Be flawless or be attacked. Professor Porter chose to be flawless. And that made me want to vomit.

She asked a small group of us how we were enjoying 1L year, which is what they call the first year of law school. It's elitism and nothing else.

"We're really scared of you," confessed my classmate Emily. I didn't know her well, but at this point I decided I loved her.

Professor Porter just stared at Emily blankly, and then unleashed a forced laugh. There was something very algorithmic about her. Beep. Boop. Beep.

Soon after the barbecue, I learned Emily was a Bravo TV fan. I am a Bravo superfan and have, on more than one occasion, been deemed "Bravosexual." (And I resent the notion that reality TV is "trash," as if *The Big Bang Theory* is High Art.)

Except Emily didn't actually watch the shows. Instead, she read Julie Klausner's *New York* magazine recaps religiously, typically in class, which I thought was a cute personality quirk. She got me into the recaps, which I often found as enjoyable—if not more enjoyable—as the episodes themselves. I mean, the recaps were certainly more interesting than anything a court had written. Emily and I started spending the lectures in the back row reading Julie. I'd found a friend.

My childhood friend Amber started law school at Georgetown at the same time I started at Berkeley.

When we had taken Civil Liberties during our senior year of high school, we would go on jogs, debate cases, and imagine being in law school one day. Amber was always more

certain about wanting to be a lawyer than I was. She didn't
just have a lawyer father, like me, but also a lawyer mother
and a lawyer stepmother. Becoming a lawyer was a no-brainer
for her.

From Amber's stories, Georgetown seemed a lot different from
Berkeley. The differences felt classically East Coast versus West,
Vivian versus Elle. Amber's experience with law school seemed
much more stereotypically intense, the way it was portrayed in
movies like *Legally Blonde* and *The Paper Chase*. At Georgetown,
study groups were a *huge deal*. You had to be invited into the
right one or it was social suicide.

If this was the case at Berkeley, I did not notice. Emily,
Spencer, and I haphazardly assembled a study group with a few
others from our mod. I'd befriended Spencer after he charged
into our Legal Research and Writing class ranting about the
terrible AT&T service in Berkeley. I wasn't sure if he was
talking to me or just the air, but I loved his anger—it was a
refreshing break from my classmates who acted like we were
all on some sort of stage performing or were being closely
monitored. He looked right at me and asked, "Do you have
AT&T?"

"I do." I nodded. "It's terrible."

He smiled. We were friends. And with Emily, we became a
trio that would get me through my first semester. Our study
group would meet in rented conference rooms, chug Diet Coke,
and gossip about our professors.

Amber said at Georgetown people snorted amphetamines in
the restrooms to perform better in class. To me, amphetamines
were a party drug. They made me feel euphoric, and I definitely
wouldn't waste that high on *class*. I spent most classes in the

back row scrolling *Olsens Anonymous*, my favorite Olsen Twin fan blog.

At Berkeley, weed brownies were served at campus events. We popped Molly like gum. Neither are performance-enhancing drugs.

Before law school, I'd always been good at school. I am an anxious person, but school was not something that stressed me out. It was my happy place. Unlike other areas of my life, school was a manageable and controllable universe. I did what the teacher wanted and I was rewarded with an A. I graduated undergrad with a 3.94 GPA. My main complaint with college was that it was not challenging enough.

I know.

I was excited to be intellectually challenged at a good school where good grades really meant something. And I mostly enjoyed the experience.

I loved playing beer pong with people who were smarter than me. I loved reading weird, archaic cases filled with bizarre, pretentious language. I loved going into the grand air-conditioned library with its big windows that overlooked the bay, watching the fog roll over the Golden Gate Bridge at sunset.

People say there is an impossible amount of reading in law school, which I didn't find to be remotely true. Most courses assigned roughly thirty pages per lecture, which is an easy amount to skim. I'd perfected this practice in high school, where I'd gotten good grades through a combination of skimming and SparkNotes. The key is to read for the takeaway, for something to say in class when called on, but not to obsess over whether you're retaining every detail. That's a waste of time. The obsessing should come during exam time, when it matters. Until then, skimming the textbooks and reading case summaries online do just fine.

I enjoyed my law school skimming. I got a kick out of all the phallic language, like *dicta*, a court's opinion considered authoritative but not binding; *subpoena*, a writ summoning a person to court; and *penal*, prescribing punishment.

I loved the random strings of Latin, like *res ipsa loquitur*, which means "the thing speaks for itself."

I loved learning all the exceptions to the *hearsay rule*, or the rule prohibiting secondhand statements from being used as evidence at trial. There are a whopping twenty-three exceptions to the rule. My favorite was the "dying declaration," a statement made by someone under a belief of certain or impending death. The original idea behind the rule was that the speaker was closer to God and therefore less likely to lie. I doubted the efficacy of this exception. Wouldn't the best time to lie be when you're on the brink of escaping any possible accountability, forever?

I loved it all even more when I was high. When the anxiety about whether or not I fully grasped the concepts faded, I was tickled by the peculiarity of it all.

I became obsessed with the *reasonable man* standard, which is used mostly to determine whether someone acted negligently in torts.

This hypothetical reasonable person exercises the average care and judgment that society requires to protect this individual's own and others' interests. In determining whether a defendant was negligent, you measure the defendant's conduct in relation to that of a reasonable person in similar circumstances.

As soon as I read about torts, I called up my college friend

Henry. "We need to be careful about getting sued for negligence." I went on to explain the reasonable man standard, and how it might pose a problem for us in light of our drinking habits.

"If you're going to go out," I said, "just make sure you're around someone richer than you so if you accidentally trip someone and they crack their head open, they'll sue him instead of you." I paused. "Or *her.*" I was becoming a feminist.

Torts made me paranoid.

Whenever we had a break—we had tons of random breaks for no reason—I'd drive to LA. LA was a far cry from DC, with all the stuffy politicos and government workers, and SF, with its neo-hippie technocrats. LA had movie stars! For one trip, I downloaded a lecture that was supposed to teach me about torts. It included a whole section on things flying off delivery trucks and killing people. So, during the entire drive, I imagined my death.

It was around this time that I also started speaking in A, B, C terms, mimicking the orderly thought process drilled into us in law school.

Well, I don't want sushi for dinner: (A) I read that white rice spikes insulin, and I'm not trying to get diabetes anytime soon. (B) The oceans are polluted as hell, and I don't want mercury poisoning. And (C) I'm craving cheese.

If someone had a different opinion, I'd come at them with another A, B, C. *You want Italian? Well, I don't think that's in your best interests. (A) There is no Italian immigrant population in Berkeley, so it won't be authentic. (B) Authenticity is the spice of life, and dinner;) And (C) gluten is canceled.*

In addition to becoming overly methodical, my communication became even more antagonistic than normal, which

45

annoyed everyone around me. Nobody was that interested in my reasoning behind dinner decisions, or literally anything else.

But my new communication style was helpful for my side hustle as a rapper. It sounds inane, I know. But instead of just listening to them, I started writing raps. I think this happens to anyone when they have enough THC in their system.

I think.

Truth be told, rap and the law aren't actually that different. They're both antagonistic (I'm right, you're wrong) and solipsistic (my point of view is all that exists). They're both rooted in social unrest. My practice in one seemed to feed off the other, and vice versa. I was becoming bossy, assertive, and persuasive as hell.

I started getting into rap battles via text message with my college friend Liv, another academic overachiever working on her master's at Yale. In one exchange, I asked her "advanced degree to suck my JD." Suffice it to say, I was the coolest person in law school. Or maybe I was the biggest loser. It's a fine line.

———

Lots of people talk about how rigorous law school is, but not enough people talk about how *messy* it is. I recently spoke to another lawyer about this book, and she was delighted. "More people need to be talking about that shit." She launched into a story of how her classmates spilled cocaine all over the floor of the bar at "law prom." She forwarded me the email the administration had sent out following the incident. Of note:

By 10:30, some guests started engaging in behavior that we can characterize only as completely reprehensible. Someone dropped a glass from a height of several stories down a stairwell, putting others in serious danger. Management informed us that an individual went into a kitchen and urinated there before exiting the building.

By 11, another glass had dropped from a similar height. An unidentified white powder exploded over the third floor.

The unidentified white-powder explosion felt poetic.

Another favorite story came from my friend Leia, a law student in DC, who told me her classmate sucked a guy's dick in a fourth-floor study room with glass walls that exposed them to the rest of campus. The epitome of romance. Unfortunately, her classmate was soon humiliated because his dick didn't get hard. Leia, a lesbian, clarified that she—like me—became nauseated hearing the details. "Her reaction to this was to go to the gym every day so he might get hard next time."

That classic law student willpower!

Granted, law school's not all blow and blow jobs. I did spend *some* time studying. To study, we made outlines. Berkeley Law Academic Support Services circulated a handout encouraging us to make outlines in order to "think systematically about the subject, or rather, how to 'think like a lawyer.'" It's essentially an attempt to reduce all the materials from a course—cases, statutes, general principles—into their simplest forms.

The handout also said there was "nothing magical about it except the process of doing it," which comforted me because my outlines were not magical. But I enjoyed making them. I

47

would go to the library, crack open a Diet Coke, blast Aphex Twin in my headphones, and start typing. To this day, I'm always looking for ways to organize a chaotic and overwhelming universe into something more systematic and under control. It's probably why I write books and take online IQ tests when I'm bored. (Confession: my IQ is just above average.)

Most law school exams are "issue spotters." You're given several complex fact patterns and are tasked with identifying every potential legal issue that could arise. It doesn't matter how many cases or legal rules you've memorized. Spotting issues—or potential legal questions raised by the specific facts of a dispute—is the only way to score points. Issues include questions of which law applies, how a law applies, or whether a law applies at all. We answered using something called CREAC:

- Conclusion (how the court will likely rule, including alternative outcomes created by ambiguities in the facts)
- Rule (relevant statutes and case law)
- Explanation (how courts apply the rules)
- Application (applying the relevant rules to the facts, comparing and contrasting relevant cases, analyzing and distinguishing)
- Conclusion (restate)

My boyfriend Charlie's outlines were much prettier and more organized than mine. He also got much better grades. I'm not sure if these things are related. His IQ was well above average. When he emailed me his Torts outline, he wrote: "I think this covers every page of reading in the class." Looking back, I understand why I had a crush on him. He was such a good student!

Some courses allowed us to use outlines during the test. When this was the case, we made "attack outlines." They were shorter and designed for referencing under the pressure of a ticking clock. It sounds like having an outline during the test would make it easier, but since we were graded on a curve, it didn't do much but create a lot of frantic page flipping during the exam.

Aside from making outlines, we would form study groups and take old exams together in stuffy law school conference rooms. Take, for example, the following Torts hypothetical.

Davy, a dog breeder, wanted to sell some puppies. Mick and Janet went over to look at the puppies in Davy's living room. Davy warned them not to go into the room at the end of the hall. Janet reached into the puppy pen and one of the puppies bit her hand. Davy told Mick to go to the bathroom near the end of the hall to get some Band-Aids.

Forgetting Davy's warning, Mick opened the door at the end of the hall. He'd mistaken it for the bathroom. Inside the room was a huge chimpanzee, which jumped between Mick and the door and began beating its chest.

Attending to Janet's bite, Davy mistakenly grabbed a bottle of heavy-duty solvent, thinking it was antiseptic. When Davy rubbed the solution into Janet's wound, she began to scream in pain. Hearing these cries, Mick charged past the chimpanzee, which gave him a huge gash to the head as he passed. Shaken, Mick and Janet fled Davy's house. Afterward, they filed suit to recover for their injuries.

I would have fun frantically writing down causes of actions and potential defenses as fast as I could. *Was Davy negligent in exposing Janet to the puppy that bit her? What duty of care did he owe her in his own home? Did he breach it?* I'd break down each of these scenarios—duty, breach, causation, damages— produce a ton of words, and feel confident, ready to show off. But once we started discussing it, I'd realize I'd just grazed the surface. I'd oversimplified things and left a billion things out.

My friends would go much deeper, spotting issues I hadn't even thought of. They'd discuss strict liability, that the owner of a wild animal is strictly liable for any injuries caused by the animal's dangerous propensities. They'd discuss comparative negligence, or the idea that Janet's own negligence in reaching into the pen and Mick's negligence in failing to heed Davy's warning would reduce their total recovery by the percentage of their own negligence compared to Davy's.

I loved being wowed by my friends' brains.

Then we would read the sample answer and realize there were issues none of us had spotted. We'd forgotten to discuss assumption of the risk, or whether Janet voluntarily assumed the risk of a bite by reaching into the playpen, or whether Mick voluntarily assumed risk when he walked into the chimp room. We'd forgotten to address the extent of the damages, that Janet would be entitled to medical expenses, pain and suffering, and lost past and future earnings if the dog bite caused her to miss work or reduced her ability to work.

This shit was always harder than it seemed.

After my first semester, I was shocked and appalled by my grades, which we didn't receive until we had returned from winter break. We didn't have a traditional grading system. We were graded on a curve. The top 10 percent of the class was awarded High Honors (HH). The next 30 percent got Honors (H). And the remaining 60 percent got Pass (P). That meant that the majority of my classmates, people like me who had gotten nothing but As their entire lives, many at Ivy League colleges, would get the lowest possible grade.

I'd never heard of anyone failing, but the school maintained it was possible. I heard it only happened if you didn't show up to the test or just handed in a blank page. If you showed up and wrote something down, you would pass.

"P-slapped," Emily said to me in the hallway when we got back to campus.

"P-slapped," I said back to her.

Neither of us had actually been P-slapped. We'd both received Hs—me in Civil Procedure and Legal Writing; Emily in Civil Procedure and Torts. But we received Ps in the other subjects— me in Criminal Law and Torts; Emily in Criminal Law and Legal Writing—and we were overachievers, so two Hs wasn't good enough. All we saw were the Ps—the worst possible score, the score you received simply for showing up and trying. *Two* of them. Worst of all, in Criminal Law. How could I get a fucking P in Criminal Law when I had spent an entire year's internship writing criminal defense motions and briefs to an actual court? And *won* one! But the skills it takes to write successful briefs and motions are different from those needed to ace an issue spotter. Most notably, with briefs and motions you have *time*. You also have mentors, colleagues, and the internet at your fingertips. An issue spotter is similar to a standardized test. It's all about how quickly your brain and your brain alone can connect ideas under pressure. And apparently my brain worked better with Wi-Fi access.

I went to Charlie's and cried and cried. "I think I'm going to drop out," I moaned.

"Anna," he said to me. "You know you go to the same school as *me*?" This was his way of making me feel better. It was comically condescending, and yet, like the masochist I am, I was falling in love with him.

———————

I had met Charlie at the very first "Bar Review" of 1L year. The name is a stupid pun for a weekly event where law students convene at a local bar, drink away the week's stress, and plant the seeds for a lifelong unhealthy relationship with alcohol.[1] I went to *every single Bar Review* in law school.

As with most men I've dated, I originally thought Charlie was gay.

We met in a bar called Pappy's on Telegraph Avenue. I was so excited for the first Bar Review, hyped to get drunk and *discuss ideas* with people who were smarter than me. I pregamed alone in my sad studio because I didn't have any friends yet and then walked up to Telegraph.

In the crowded bar, Charlie immediately approached and started chatting me up. He seemed pretty drunk. "Why aren't you drinking a *real* drink?" he asked, eyeing my beer.

"I only drink beer," I said. It was true, a very embarrassing personal fact. It's what I grew up drinking and it was the only alcohol that really did it for me. Wine made me nauseous; hard liquor made me sad. Beer made me happy and chatty. Whereas these people terrified me in the sterile law school hallways, I felt very confident sipping a beer and chatting with them in this corny sports bar. As long as I had a cold beer in my hands, I could talk to anyone.

"Lame," he said, and walked away. I don't remember who else I talked to that night. I remember Charlie came back later with a beer and spilled a little bit of it on me. "Sorry," he said. "I have my period."

I laughed.

"Just because I don't really know ya," he said, in a sort of dorky Jewish rapper voice, "doesn't mean I can't bleed upon ya."

I laughed really hard; I have no idea why. I thought it was so funny that I took out my phone and tweeted it. (I must have been really drunk.) I asked him for his handle to properly give him credit, even though I had only, like, twenty followers. I had, and have, a compulsive desire to put everything I find funny or interesting into writing immediately. It's mostly a humiliating habit, but it came in handy in law school, when I had to write down everything my professors said very quickly in class.

"I wish I'd brought a joint," Charlie mused.

I nearly started salivating. I normally kept a bowl and a grinder filled with weed in my Marc by Marc purse at all times, but I'd left it at home. I was trying to be "professional," or something. But whenever I started drinking, I wanted weed. Later I would move onto wanting other things, too—uppers, etc.—but at that point, I was young and pure.

"I have weed at my house!" I practically shouted. I wanted to smoke so bad. I wanted to get high with this funny, smart, gay man in my new studio—the very first apartment I'd had to myself, which I'd decorated with palm plants and the afore-mentioned black-light poster of Biggie Smalls. "It's just around the corner."

He agreed. In my studio, I put on A$AP Rocky and we smoked a bowl and chatted. He'd gone to Harvard undergrad and had gotten into Harvard Law but didn't want to go back there. This was cool to me, that he'd turned down Harvard Law. I didn't have any friends who had gone to Harvard, let alone turned it down.

We commiserated about not having gotten into Stanford Law. *No one*, we agreed, got into Stanford Law. Then he tried to kiss me. I backed away. I was shocked. I thought he was gay. I felt a little confused for a few days, but then when he asked me out over Gchat a few days later, I was excited.

I have a crush, I texted my best friend from high school.

Charlie made me laugh and smoked weed and had a degree from Harvard, which apparently was all I needed at twenty-three years old to become obsessed with someone. Dating him was fun because it was kind of like dating an encyclopedia; he knew everything and hardly ever emoted. My high mind would wander and he'd be able to meet me wherever it ended up— economic theory, Radiohead's discography, aliens . . . whatever. He knew everything about everything. He was high basically all the time, and he still scored perfectly on every test. He had scored a 180 on the LSAT. It was sick.

———

By this point, it's likely crystal clear I have masochistic tendencies. I have all this privilege I did nothing to deserve. Punishing myself always felt like a way to even the score. It was the least I could do.

My first-semester Ps do not seem like a big deal at all, not even to me in retrospect, but at the time, it was hell. At that time, grades were the only thing I ever cried about. Sometimes I cried in movies, like when I went to see *Precious* with Fernando. But mostly I cried about grades. If it wasn't the best one I could get, I felt it said something horrible about me. It was definitive proof I was worthless. It is this exact twisted line of thinking that compels people to go to law school and that keeps them trapped in the profession for life.

After getting P-slapped (ish), it was clear I was not going to be at the top of my class, which devastated me. Your first-year grades mattered the most—because they were how law firms made hiring decisions—and I'd already botched the first semester. I started getting more Hs and HHs as time went on, but I would never recover from those initial Ps.

The people who got the top grades frightened me. They were skittish and frail, with tired eyes and thinning hair, and a clear aversion to mascara. Sometimes I'd catch them pacing outside of the library late at night with a cigarette—ostensibly their only vice—as I was leaving my weed dealer's frat house. The other people who got top grades were Charlie types, socially peculiar and abnormally good at test taking. Total freaks of nature.

I didn't realize my best friend Spencer was among them until OCI, the on-campus interview week, when all the top law firms came to interview us in hotel rooms for summer jobs. Spencer was basically being stalked. Watching him get cornered by various big-deal attorneys in the hotel hallways, I felt a sort of pride that he'd decided to be my friend. I liked him even more after that, and I already liked him a lot. I remember people always assumed we were dating, which I didn't correct, even though he was gay and I had a boyfriend (and I was also gay).

Spencer later went on to work for David Boies, among the most famous litigators in the country. Boies won the file-sharing case that pushed Napster into bankruptcy. He represented Al Gore in *Bush v. Gore*. He represented Harvey Weinstein and Theranos. And he represented the plaintiff in *Hollingsworth v. Perry*, which invalidated California Proposition 8 banning same-sex marriage.

Anyway, I couldn't compete with freaks like Spencer and Charlie and the girls who slept in the library, so I had to find a new identity to occupy. I could no longer be Anna—a little cold but very good at school. Instead, I decided I'd become something I'd wanted to be my whole life.

In law school, I got to be Dumb & Hot.

CHAPTER 5

Clueless

In *Clueless*, Cher Horowitz argues her way into good grades.

In their Beverly Hills home one night, Cher's father asks her, "You mean to tell me that you argued your way from a C plus to an A minus?"

Cher responds, eager to please her scary litigator father: "Totally based on my powers of persuasion. You proud?"

"Honey," her dad says, "I couldn't be happier than if they were based on real grades."

This scene really inspired me.

After watching *Clueless* a second time in high school, I started questioning my teachers whenever I received less than an A. I'd show up in their office and demand an explanation. I'd argue that my test answers were more correct than they initially thought. Even in math and science, I would argue that although my answer might have been technically incorrect, I deserved full credit for my work because I'd shown that I had mastered the concepts. I told them that my mistakes were too small and insignificant to affect my grade.

So, when I got to law school, the Socratic method didn't scare me like it did my classmates. For those who haven't seen *Legally Blonde*, the Socratic method is the prevailing pedagogical technique used in law school. The professor fires a series of questions at you to highlight the flaws in your argument and thereby to arrive at some kind of greater truth. The idea of being interrogated by our professors without warning compelled most of my classmates to do the reading three times over to ensure they wouldn't embarrass themselves in a room of ninety, otherwise known as our large mod.

I wasn't concerned: I can bullshit.

But I will never forget the first time the Socratic method was used on me, because it was during my very first law school class ever. I arrived late because I had been stung by a bee on the walk to class. As I was rushing to my seat in the lecture hall, the terrifying Professor Nicole Porter called on me without warning. This is a lynchpin of the Socratic method, the "cold call."

"Ms. Dorn," she said while I scrambled over my cohorts. "What is 'reasonable doubt'?"

I desperately wanted to answer "Jay-Z's best album," but I bit my tongue and regurgitated the definition from the reading.

Afterward, people kept coming up to me in the halls and telling me I did a good job. I didn't think much of it because, honestly, who doesn't know what reasonable doubt is?

But there were lots of times I was called on and had no idea what the answer was and could make something up. But not in Contracts.

(I've never read a contract, ever, not once. And I never will. Life is too short!)

Professor Bergen was particularly obtuse, and I never had any idea what the fuck he was talking about. Luckily, I had Emily. In between Julie Klausner recaps, we spent the lectures tallying how often the first-row suck-ups raised their overeager hands.

Once Professor Bergen cold-called me, and I pretended I wasn't there.

I was sitting in the back row, and everyone turned to look at me.

"Ms. Dorn?" the professor said several times.

Everyone just kept staring at me, but I remained still and silent.

I didn't know the answer, so I attempted a different type of power move: strategic withholding.

Finally, the professor moved on.

I wasn't too worried given it was allegedly nearly impossible to fail a class. When it came to finals time second semester, I cut my losses and didn't study for Contracts at all. I studied hard for the other classes. And still got P-slapped. (And by that I mean I got two Hs but could only see the Ps, the passes, the lowest grade.)

By the end of 1L year, I knew enough to stay away from any business-related class. You know, the classes that taught subjects and skills that could eventually make me money? Not for me! Instead, I took classes in critical race and gender theory in which we examined how the law was bad or ineffective in abstract terms—obviously my shit.

———

During 2L year—second year in inane lawyer speak—Spencer and I became teaching assistants for Professor Kelly, who taught Legal Research and Writing (LRW) and Written and Oral Advocacy (WOA).

Kelly taught our small mod for LRW during 1L year, and Spencer and I worshipped her. (We called our legal writing instructors by their first names for reasons that, to me, felt primarily sexist because *all* the legal writing instructors were women.) Kelly was one of the few law instructors I found remotely aspirational. She ran the Legal Writing Department, wore athleisure most days, and posted a lot of photos on Facebook of herself drinking tequila at her kids' soccer games. Early in our "professional relationship," I accidentally signed my name "Anya" in an email to her. And she jokingly called me that for months.

Also, LRW was the only class in which I felt remotely confident. Legal writing came naturally to me.

The primary LRW assignment is writing a legal memorandum in response to a legal question proposed by a fictional law firm superior. Ours involved whether the "English-Only Policy" at a fictional chain restaurant called "Spun Steak" was legally permissible.

We used CREAC (conclusion, rule, explanation, application, and conclusion) to answer the question. We looked up cases and predicted how the court would rule by comparing those cases, and the rules announced therein, to our facts at hand.

Kelly broke the class into two groups: one half was tasked with arguing the policy was legally permissible, and the other half was tasked with arguing it wasn't. This way, we weren't expected to determine which side was "correct" but rather to argue a predetermined position, simulating what lawyers do for their clients.

We also had to argue our side in front of a fictional judge, which was nerve-racking but exciting. I ended up getting an Honors in the class, and Kelly said that I seemed "cool, calm, and collected" during my oral argument—a major compliment because most of my energy goes into appearing calmer than I really am.

That said, I was upset I didn't win the 1L "Best Oralist Award," which—to absolutely no one's shock—Spencer won.

As we heard Spencer's little acceptance speech, Emily whispered under her breath, "I've won 'Best Oralist' before . . . but it had nothing to do with law."

I cackled.

The next year, when Spencer and I TA'd, our 1L students had a sexier assignment than Spun Steak. Theirs was based on the Woody Allen lawsuit against American Apparel. The then trendy clothing company had posted billboards around Los Angeles and New York using an image of Allen from *Annie Hall* without Allen's permission. Our students were given fairly similar facts. Half the class had to argue that American Apparel illegally used Allen's likeness, and the other half had to argue it was fair use.

The most alarming aspect of the whole thing was that a lot of our students had never heard of Woody Allen.

Their cultural blindness saddened me, and I told them to go home and watch *Manhattan*.

Sometimes, we'd have TA "office hours." I think students mostly came to see Spencer. Once, Spencer called out sick and all the students left when they saw it was just me there. But I got a huge high when my students actually took me seriously. Mostly because they were all older and smarter than me. It was super fun telling thirty-year-olds who had graduated from Ivy League schools that they didn't know how to write. I've always gotten a high from telling people they are wrong. It's not something I like about myself, but it came in handy as a TA. And it's why writing briefs, which are adversarial in nature, came naturally to me.

The biggest high, though, came at the end of the semester, when Spencer and I got to play mock judges for the oral portion of the students' assignment. The oral arguments were held in the Ninth Circuit Court of Appeals in San Francisco, a granite and marble beaux arts building constructed in 1905, truly opulent and grandiose. I wore a judicial robe and sat on the bench behind a placard that said "Judge Dorn." In the palatial courtroom, I fired questions at the students designed to undermine their arguments and force them to articulate counterpoints.

I've never felt more glamorous and powerful in my entire life.

I felt like Marie Fucking Antoinette!

The problem was that 1L students are *very* nervous and extremely sensitive. At one point I asked a student a question and she stumbled over the answer, clearly not having prepared for the point I was nudging her toward. Afterward, she stormed out of the courtroom crying.

I felt bad for making her cry, but more than that I felt she needed to toughen up. Lawyers look down on these sorts of emotional displays, and I was no exception. My tendency to turn cold and unflinching when I'm under attack always made me feel somewhat superior and helped me tremendously in the law.

In my personal life, it has been less useful.

The worst part of TA'ing was when students asked me about *The Bluebook*, the unduly complicated style manual for legal citations. I took a very improvisational approach to citations. Whenever a student asked me about *The Bluebook*, I'd tell them to figure it out themselves.

"I won't be there to help at your summer internship," I'd say with a wink.

I acted like I was doing them a favor, but really I had no fucking idea how to cite anything, and didn't care to learn. *The Bluebook* was like the stock market to me. I know it exists. I've read about it a billion times and had people explain it to me over and over again. I do not get it. All I hear is words.

My inability to master *The Bluebook* didn't prevent me from doing well in my legal writing classes, nor did it hurt me in my career as a lawyer. I felt like as long as I was "close enough"—in other words, not egregiously off base—I would be fine, and I was mostly right about that. Instead of consulting *The Bluebook*, I would look at how cases were cited in legal opinions and loosely copy them. I realized from this experiment that judges didn't really understand *The Bluebook* either, because their citations were all over the place. The discrepancies could be chalked up to the fact that different jurisdictions had different rules, but even within the same jurisdictions, I noticed glaring inconsistencies.

Minus the citations, legal writing was really fun. Sometimes I even miss it. It's much more straightforward than creative writing, and there is no expectation for your words to be entertaining or accessible to mass audiences. You can be as rude and dull and pretentious as you want. And I enjoyed arguing that my side was right. In true lawyer fashion, I didn't concern myself too much with what was fair or correct. I rather relished exploiting rhetoric to make my side *sound* correct, just like I do all damn day in conversation, annoying everyone around me.

Given my natural aptitude for written and oral argument, and the expectation that law students partake in extracurriculars in order to secure employment later, I auditioned for something called the Board of Advocates. After delivering a mock oral argument and handing in a sample brief during the end of my 1L year, I was accepted onto the appellate team. They placed me in the National Moot Court Competition along with two teammates—Greg and Hayley—to compete in during my 2L year.

Greg was a former policy debate champion (they talk really, *really* fast; google it). He was *very* competitive, a trait slightly offset by his laidback, Midwestern disposition. He was from Kansas, with hair the color of a cornfield and eyes like a cloudless plains sky.

Hayley had an innocuously pretty, symmetrical face. But her face betrayed her: she was bizarre. She was a far cry from the typical hyperalert law school woman. I think she was from Phoenix. Her attitude toward the whole thing was similar to mine, that is, *I was told I need to do extracurriculars, so here I am.*

For the competition, we were tasked with drafting briefs based on an assigned fact pattern. We'd then have to argue both sides before a fake Supreme Court.

The contrived—and abridged—facts of our case were as follows:

Tim Larson and Kelly Boyd were star students at Betterly Hills High. Boyd felt threatened by Larson's academic success and accused him on her blog of cheating on a history quiz. The blog post created a stir. The school investigated and concluded that Larson didn't cheat. Boyd was punished. Soon after, in the press, Betterly Hills teacher Tasha Welch accused Boyd of being a "documented" cheater. Boyd filed suit against the school district for violation of her First Amendment rights and against Welch and the school district for defamation.

During the investigation, when Boyd's attorneys served the school district for all emails between Welch and other teachers, Welch claimed to have deleted the emails because she "needed free space." Before trial, Boyd requested an adverse inference instruction, a type of court sanction that allows jurors to *infer* that a party who destroys evidence did so because it was unfavorable to their case. In this scenario, the instruction would permit the jury to assume that Welch's deleted emails would have shown she made false statements to the press in bad faith. The District Court granted the request and instructed the jury accordingly. The jury returned a verdict for Boyd on both her First Amendment claim and her defamation claim.

My team was tasked with representing the school district and Ms. Welch on certiorari to the "US Supreme Court."

First, we wrote a fifty-five-page brief answering these questions in a way that would support Boyd's case. I was assigned the less sexy portion—spoliation (i.e., destruction) of evidence. I am certain I will never forget the word *spoliation* for the rest of my life. In fact, until writing this book, I'd forgotten the facts of the case entirely, but I will never forget the word *spoliation*.

It sounds like an expensive skincare product or the rate at which milk goes bad. The word references "spoiling" evidence, but it doesn't actually have the word *spoil* in it—even though all logic says it should.

The word is a perfect example of how lawyers take things that should be straightforward and turn them into something that makes no sense, simply to be on the inside of knowing. *Torts* is another great example. The word alone frightens nonlawyers. But it's just personal injury law. Ambulance chasers. Those billboards you see on the freeway? Those lawyers are doing torts. And it's not that hard. Duty, breach, causation, damages—that's all it is!

The cursed *Bluebook* is filled with ways to make the law inaccessible to nonlawyers. That's what the law is all about—making what should be accessible esoteric to keep lawyer salaries high.

But I enjoyed writing the brief for the competition, which I did at my own pace from the quiet comfort of the library. I had fun researching cases and scanning them for language that would make my point sound correct—like it was the only answer. Like the other side was stupid for even *considering* that another option could be correct.

The oral portion was less fun. Unlike Emily, I'd never won any awards for my oral skills. . . .

For the oral argument, we had to argue both sides of each point. Hayley and I each took a side of the spoliation issue, while Greg argued both sides of the First Amendment issue. As a garden-variety overachiever, Greg was amped for the challenge of arguing both sides of the more complicated issue.

While Greg oozed adrenaline, Hayley and I exuded apathy at

best, hostility at worst. We wore sweatpants and rolled our eyes when our coaches gave us feedback.

My feedback tended to be stylistic. I was "overly casual" and "insufficiently deferential." I needed to insert more "your honors" and stand up straighter. (My idea of a "power pose" is hunched over and afraid. I have the posture of a crow.)

Hayley's criticism was more substantive. She was a self-proclaimed procrastinator and tended to be grossly unprepared. I often wondered why she decided to do moot court instead of mock trial. In moot court, you argue in front of a panel of judges, not a jury. It's nerdier and more intellectual, whereas mock trial is sexier and more theatrical. When you see law on TV—*Law & Order, The Practice, The Good Wife*, etc.—that's typically trial. Trial is all about facts, meaning, *What happened?* Appeals, or appellate law, are about the law—*Were legal procedures properly adhered to at trial or in the lower courts?* (It's inarguably less sexy.) When you think of cases being argued before the Supreme Court—that's appellate law.

Put simply, I thought Hayley was too hot and dumb for moot court. And I envied her for it. After all, I'd decided hot and dumb was *my* role. Greg was obviously the team genius. So who was I supposed to be? The mediocre one? No thanks!

One day, Hayley walked into practice and announced, "I'm so over this shit." We'd never explicitly discussed our disdain for these practices, and I was thrilled to have a partner in my misery.

"*Same,*" I said. "I'm sick of being scrutinized by these losers," I said, referring to our lame-ass coaches, straight men who wore chinos.

Hayley lit up. "Same!" she squealed. "They are no fun at all.

I sort of want to just fuck with them and go up there with a weird accent." She giggled and morphed into a big-haired Texan. "*Ladies and gentlemen of the jury . . .*"

I laughed at this, not only because it was funny but also because there was no jury in this competition, confirming my belief that Hayley was maybe dumb and definitely better suited for mock trial. Hell, maybe she thought this *was* mock trial.

It took a few more practices, but Hayley did indeed try her bizarre Southern accent at the podium. It took me by complete surprise, and I choked to conceal my laughter.

"Wait," one coach asked. "Hayley, is this how you plan to speak in the actual competition?"

He looked angry. The coaches were not remotely amused, which made me laugh even harder. I hid inside my American Apparel hoodie and took deep breaths to calm down.

"No," she said. "I do not."

"Okay," the coach said. "Let's get serious then."

The weekend before the actual competition, Hayley invited Greg and me over to practice. She was wearing her usual sweatsuit, drinking from a two-liter bottle of Dr. Pepper, and instantly confessed to being on "a lot of Ritalin."

A few minutes into our practice, she pulled a hookah stem from under her dining room table and took a big hit. "It calms me down," she said through a cloud of berry-scented smoke before offering the stem to us. We both shook our heads. I wanted to say yes, mostly to cement my allyship with the lackadaisical Hayley over the rigid Greg. But I didn't think I could make myself work on the law with a hookah buzz. Once buzzed, law was the last thing I wanted to think about. I would just be texting my friends and scrolling *Olsens Anonymous*.

By the time the actual competition came around, I was beyond over it. My biggest fear was that we would make it to the next round. I wanted to lose gracefully and get the hell out of there.

The competition was at UC Hastings in San Francisco, the law school across the bay. I felt embarrassed as soon as I entered the building. I'd never been in a room with so many nerds per square foot in my life. When I got into the elevator, someone said in a sing-song voice, *"It's the most wonderful time of the year!"*

I forced a weak smile.

It was annoying when people said this about Christmas, but it was truly deranged to say it about the beginning of a moot court competition.

Luckily, my wish came true. We lost the competition in the first round.

And it wasn't because I messed up. It was mostly Hayley, and the fact that the people we competed against seemed to be robots. Apparently, Berkeley's teams didn't practice nearly as hard as the teams from other schools did, which was confounding, because I couldn't imagine spending more time and energy on this competition than I already had. I felt like I deserved a paycheck.

The team we lost to could recite the record and case law as though these were imprinted on their brains. They spoke in robotic voices and moved mechanically; I kept wondering whether I would catch them shoving USB cords up their asses during the break to recharge.

The judges echoed my coaches' feedback, saying that my demeanor was "inappropriately casual." But one judge said my presentation was "cool." I kept waiting for him to ask me out afterward, but he never did.

Greg was livid when we lost.

"This competition is bullshit," he said. I agreed, but not for the same reason. Greg thought it was bullshit because the judges didn't notice the winners had miscited the law, which of course I did not notice either. I thought it was bullshit because arguing was bullshit, childish, and a very silly way to mediate disputes.

Of course, arguing to mediate disputes is the whole point of law, which begged the question: Why was I in law school? I didn't have an answer.

This was a fake case, anyway. Who cared? It all felt very pointless. Moot court is inherently low stakes, but people were acting like it was high stakes and had lost sight of the actual difference between high and low stakes while turning everything into an intellectual exercise in a vacuum. Again: Why was I in law school? Still no answer.

There was no art to it! Nothing smart, valuable, or aspirational about it.

"Let's go get drunk," I said, and we did.

But unfortunately, I couldn't get Greg to stop complaining about the competition I wanted to forget that night.

We never hung out again.

I didn't speak to Hayley again until 3L year when we took a class together and she asked me for a copy of my paper to "reference." I let her! Honestly, I was flattered.

Overall, the moot court competition was a microcosmic representation of my time at Berkeley Law. I didn't win, but I didn't lose either. I didn't attract unwanted attention. I did fine. I was adequate. I made absolutely no impact.

When push came to shove, my favorite thing about being at

Berkeley Law was telling people that I was at Berkeley Law. No matter how messy my hair was or how socially bizarre I acted, people assumed I had my shit together. I was at a top ten law school. I was thriving.

And by that I mean numb as shit.

CHAPTER 6

The Golden Handcuffs

I wasn't prepared for most aspects of law school, but in particular I had no idea that we would be expected to get summer internships. The 1L summer internship isn't nearly as important as 1L grades, which are *everything* to employers, or the 2L internship, which essentially determines the rest of your career, but the internship after your first year in law school still seemed to matter. All spring semester, my classmates were constantly talking about their 1L summer prospects, each time feeding my anxiety. My grades were average, so I figured I needed a good internship.

But I wasn't really sure what a good internship even was. In retrospect, I know that the top students interned for federal governmental agencies like the EPA, respected nonprofits like the ACLU, or federal judges.

And when it came time to find an internship, I had no idea where to look.

So I called Fernando.

"Anna," he said. "You *must* intern for a judge! I have a good relationship with Judge Button at the Hall of Justice. I can talk to her and get you an interview."

And just like that, I got the job. That is how I got pretty much every legal job I ever had. I assume my classmates got their jobs the same way—knowing people, word of mouth. A lot of them returned to places they had worked as paralegals or investigators at public defender offices or nonprofits prior to law school.

Most 1L summer internships are unpaid, which seems sort of insane given how expensive law school is.

I was annoyed I had to give away my summer to free labor, similar to how I was annoyed the moot court competition didn't come with a fat paycheck.

———————

On my first day, I met Judge Button in her chambers at San Francisco Superior Court.

The Hall of Justice is a county courthouse, meaning it's city-funded and therefore a bit run-down, but Judge Button made the best of her surroundings. In her chambers, orchids lined the windowsills, which boasted an unadulterated view of the financial district and the iconic Coca-Cola billboard.

The first thing Judge Button said to me was that I looked "healthy." She frowned when she said it, as though it were an insult.

I said that I did, in fact, like to eat healthy.

She shook her head. "That's going to be a problem." She loved barbecue, red meat, melted cheese . . . press repeat. She bought me lunch that day, and a bunch of times that summer, I supposed because the internship was unpaid. Except her taste wasn't as fancy as Fernando's. She liked dives, not yuppy enclaves.

But lunch was the least memorable thing about my first day.

My first day in Judge Button's courtroom coincided with the first day of jury selection in a homicide trial.

Dozens of potential jurors filed into the courtroom, and Judge Button told them the basic facts of the case: A homeless man had been accused of murdering his girlfriend, who was also homeless. The alleged murder took place inside a tent in the Tenderloin, a famously gritty neighborhood.

Judge Button fired questions at prospective jurors about their background and potential biases to determine whether they would be fit to serve. This process is called *voir dire*, French for "speak the truth."

I was amazed by the questions she asked and how frankly jurors answered.

Have you suffered from depression? Addiction? Have you been suicidal? Have you been the victim of a violent crime? Has a loved one been murdered?

I was depressed after my first child was born. I was addicted to cocaine in my early twenties. I attempted suicide as a teen. I was robbed at gunpoint last year. My best friend in college was murdered.

It was like this big public therapy session.

After Judge Button's questioning and weeding out of jurors deemed unable to serve, the lawyers on both sides were permitted to challenge specific jurors and possibly strike them from the jury. There are two types of strikes: *for cause* and *peremptory*.

For cause challenges are used for potential jurors the lawyer believes cannot be fair and impartial. For example, a juror who is related to one of the parties of the case cannot be objective.

Each lawyer is entitled to an unlimited number of challenges for cause, but it was ultimately up to Judge Button whether the juror would be removed from the panel.

A lawyer could use a *peremptory* challenge to have a juror struck from the panel without giving a reason, but each side has only ten. Lawyers do not need to state their reason for making a peremptory challenge, so I was left with my guesses. I noticed that the lawyers tended to strike jurors who had a lot to say during voir dire. I tell my friends who don't want to be picked for a jury to just be very opinionated during juror questioning. I assumed the lawyers figured these people would be harder to sway—that is, manipulate.

During a later internship at the Federal Public Defender office in Oakland, I asked a trial attorney what her ideal jury looked like. She told me she typically wants teachers and social workers because they tend to be liberal, have a better understanding of systemic injustice, and are more likely to be sympathetic toward her client's situation. She also said she likes engineers because they are trained to look at situations in a detached and logical way, without letting emotions interfere. They are therefore less likely to be swayed by emotionally manipulative prosecutorial narratives and more likely to focus purely on the evidence. She typically doesn't want Asians on the jury because Asians tend to be very law-and-order oriented—they are less likely to see the situation as nuanced and want to swiftly punish someone for the crime. She said this in hushed tones, like she knew it was wrong to say.

And it wasn't just wrong.

Striking jurors on the basis of race was deemed unconstitutional by the Supreme Court in *Batson v. Kentucky* in 1986. It is, of course, a very hard thing to prove, especially because lawyers aren't required to explain peremptory challenges.

If lawyers were striking jurors on the basis of race in Judge Button's courtroom, I didn't notice.

In the homeless homicide case, jury selection took over a week.

When the jury had finally been chosen, Judge Button said she was surprised the attorneys had picked juror number 7. This juror had admitted to being the victim of a stabbing and had a lot of tattoos. I asked Judge Button why she was skeptical of juror number 7; she said she "just had a feeling."

Midway through the trial, following a lunch break, Judge Button asked all jurors except for juror number 7 to exit the courtroom. The jurors obeyed. I watched the following interaction with bated breath, as though it was a television drama.

"Juror number 7," Judge Button said in a stern voice.

He nodded, looking calm.

"Are you under the influence of any drugs or alcohol at the moment?"

He shook his head.

"I need you to answer yes or no for the record."

"No," he said.

"Are you on any medication?"

He shook his head again.

"Yes or no, juror number 7." Judge Button was becoming agitated.

"No," he said.

"Are you being honest with me, juror number 7?"

He swallowed, but said nothing.

"One of my colleagues informed me that they saw you stumbling in the hallway."

He said nothing again.

"I will ask you again, juror number 7, are you under the influence of any alcohol or narcotic?"

He opened his mouth, then closed it, then opened it again. "I'm an addict." He looked down.

Judge Button's eyes opened wide and then she seemed to force herself to gain composure. "What are you addicted to?" she asked.

Juror number 7 cleared his throat. "PCP."

"Do you take it every day?"

I wanted Judge Button to end this public shaming. But it felt like she was drawing it out. A dramatic performance piece. Judges always do this. The more desperate the gallery, the longer a judge will take to get to the information everyone craves.

"Yes," he said.

"Are you on PCP today?"

He nodded. "Yes."

Both of their voices seemed to echo in the mostly empty courtroom. Judge Button looked extra high and mighty up on her bench, and juror number 7 looked extra small and alone in the jury box. Lawyers nervously shifted their papers in the gallery, and I scribbled on my notepad to look occupied.

"When did you take it?"

"This morning. Before court. And then at lunch."

"Have you been on it the whole trial?"

He nodded.

"Juror number 7, you are excused," she finally said.

I exhaled.

Boom, like that, he was gone. An alternate took his place. And the trial went on.

Juror number 7's dramatic removal took precedence in my mind over the verdict. What I took away from the experience: trial is more a performance than anything else.

The whole thing made me uneasy.

Judge Button was a former prosecutor, which Fernando had warned me about. Public defenders tended to see prosecutors as the enemy, and I'd been indoctrinated to believe the same during my internship with Fernando. Prosecutors, I'd been told, were politically conservative and morally corrupt. But Judge Button was different. She was progressive. And she had exclusively prosecuted domestic violence cases, as opposed to putting people away for nonviolent drug offenses. She was a feminist.

"I never wanted to be a judge," she told me early in the internship. "I wanted to be a romance novelist." She looked out wistfully over the orchids on her windowsill. "But my parents thought law was more practical."

I could relate, given that I, too, was an aspiring novelist who had felt compelled to go to law school. I majored in creative writing in college, but I was way too afraid to pursue it as a career. Judge Button proved what I already believed: most lawyers wanted to be something else but had caved in to the pressure of doing something safe and prestigious.

Judge Button's other intern was a sorority-type Hastings student named Stephanie who was engaged to the judge's cousin, meaning she also got the job as a personal favor. I didn't particularly like Stephanie but she seemed to like me. Or at least she liked talking at me.

That summer, I witnessed (and wrote memos regarding) three felony trials. The first was the homeless murder. The second I honestly have no memory of. The third stuck with me. A defendant had stabbed someone in the 1970s but was found "not guilty by reason of insanity." If you're found not guilty by reason of insanity in California, it's up to a jury to decide whether you're ready to be released back into the public from the mental institute where you were held. In other words, the defendant has to be found sane by a jury.

It sounds *insane*, I know.

The idea of not guilty by reason of insanity was designed to reflect society's belief that the law should not punish defendants who are mentally incapable of controlling their conduct.

California uses the M'Naghten rule to determine legal insanity, which requires that the defendant either

1. did not understand the nature of the criminal act, or
2. did not understand that what he or she was doing was morally wrong.

The rule dates back to 1840s England. It has received a lot of criticism in recent years because our understanding of mental illness has evolved significantly since the early nineteenth century. Critics point to situations in which defendants know their acts are against the law but because of their mental illness cannot control the impulses to commit them. Under the M'Naghten rule, such defendants would not be entitled to plead not guilty by reason of insanity because they knew their acts were against the law despite the fact that they committed them because of a mental illness.

Opponents to the rule propose the use of a test that addresses the defendant's cognitive abilities and better reflects contemporary understandings of mental illness. In 1972, the American Law Institute developed a new rule for insanity, which states that a defendant is not responsible for criminal conduct when he or she, as a result of mental disease or defect, does not possess the capacity either to know the conduct is criminal or to conform their conduct to the law. This rule accounts for mentally ill defendants who might know their conduct is criminal but who cannot control their conduct because of that mental illness.

Nonetheless, M'Naghten remains the standard in most states. Despite the fact that it was conceived in the 1840s, over a century before the creation of the *Diagnostic and Statistical Manual of Mental Disorders (DSM)*.

To "win" a verdict of not guilty by reason of insanity, defendants must prove that, more likely than not, they were legally insane when they committed the crime. The prize for winning this verdict is commitment to a state mental hospital. This can be worse than a guilty verdict because there is no predetermined end to the hospital commitment.

In almost all states, not guilty by reason of insanity means automatic commitment to a psychiatric facility. In most states, such as New York, no limits are placed on the duration of that commitment. In other states, such as California, limits on commitments are based on the maximum prison sentence for the underlying criminal charges. In many cases, if defendants had not pled not guilty by reason of insanity, they could have gotten out of prison earlier than they would have gotten out of the mental hospital.

This seemed like one of those cases.

Decades after his crime, this man was in Judge Button's courtroom for a jury trial to determine whether he could be released from the state hospital.

According to California Penal Code section 1026.2, the prosecution has a right to a jury trial because a restoration hearing, which determines whether the defendant's competence has been restored, has "features and indicia peculiar to a criminal action" and, thus, requires adherence to criminal procedure. In such trials, defendants have the burden of proving by a preponderance of evidence that they are no longer dangerous.

In this particular trial, a number of defense witnesses testified that the defendant, who was visibly senile and docile-looking, was not a threat to society and should have been let out a long time ago. But prosecution witnesses testified about violent incidents that had occurred during his hospital stay, such as when the defendant threatened staff or other patients, most of which seemed to have happened decades ago.

The jury hung.

That's when I gave up on the idea that trials and especially juries were anything other than inexplicable and arbitrary.

The prosecution decided it wasn't worth retrying, so luckily the defendant was freed. But where would he go? He was a senior citizen who had been locked up in a state mental hospital for three decades. Was there even a life to return to?

When the internship wasn't depressing, it was boring.

Scientific testimony was the most boring. I wasn't alone in thinking that. Judge Button *hated* scientific testimony. It was so dry and filled with seemingly inconsequential specifics.

Doctor, can you tell us your entire educational history? What certifications do you have? What articles have you published? Have you ever served on an editorial board for a scientific publication? Can you explain your current research for the jury? Has your research included human subjects in addition to animals? Have you had a chance to review documents related to this case? Did you employ evidence-based principles in reviewing this information? Are these methods/principles generally accepted in the medical field? Was a computed tomography (CT) scan performed? Was a magnetic resonance imaging (MRI) performed? Was a neurological exam performed? What is the difference between a subdural hematoma and an epidural hematoma?

This goes on and on for hours and hours.

Several times during such testimony, I caught Judge Button shopping online. She didn't even try to hide it.

Once during a homicide trial, she called me over to the bench for what I thought was a legal question. She pointed to her screen, which showed a black-and-white photo of a horse on eBay.

"Anna, should I buy it?" she asked.

"Yes," I said. "It's great."

At the end of 1L summer, most students returned to campus a few weeks early to prepare for one of the most stressful experiences in all of law school—on-campus interviewing, OCI.

As mentioned earlier, during this week, representatives from all the top law firms in the country came to Berkeley, took over the Shattuck Hotel on Telegraph Avenue, and interviewed students for their 2L summer jobs, which are said to determine the rest of our legal careers. Why? I have no idea. It was just something we all knew and all accepted.

By this point I was pretty convinced I wanted to work in criminal justice, for either the government or a nonprofit, so I wasn't planning to participate in OCI. But my parents convinced me it would be good interview practice, and I sort of liked the idea of maybe getting hired by one of these fancy firms and actually making money over the next summer. (I know that was my parents' unstated hope as well.)

And I suppose the curious side of me wanted to see what all the fuss was about.

So I signed up for a few interviews, just three or four.

Students who were gunning for firm jobs signed up for up to twenty interviews.

It was bizarre choosing which firms to interview with because they all seemed the same to me. I mostly picked firms that had offices in San Francisco, where I wanted to stay, and that boasted of their criminal defense divisions, although I knew that criminal defense in the Big Law context mostly meant white-collar crime, which is as dry as corporate law, which is as dry as paint drying.

During OCI, the Shattuck—a previously welcoming hotel where my family often stayed when they visited—morphed into an ominous place, filled with nervous energy buzzing off the walls. Students paced the lobby and hallways, mumbling their accomplishments and distinct facts about specific firms under their breath. In a suite sponsored by a law firm, which was filled with stale cookies and that firm's swag, I watched two students get into a shouting match over who was entitled to an interview slot.

I tried to act above it all, silently snickering at their lack of chill, but I was nervous, too. I didn't even *want* a law firm job. (And I was lucky enough not to have a crushing debt to worry about.) But these big-firm lawyers were so intimidating. They wanted to see vicious confidence, eagerness, and passion. I'm not good at giving off the vibe that I care, especially about an LLP.

Also, I didn't really have "the look." Before OCI, the Berkeley administration circulated a PowerPoint presentation to prepare us for interviews. Women were instructed to straighten our hair and wear heels.

I didn't own heels or a hair straightener.

Perpetually underdressed and forever aloof, I knew my appearance didn't exactly say "hire me" to a Big Law firm.

And I was right: I got no job offers. In fact, I didn't even get a callback for a second interview. Not one.

So for my 2L summer, I secured another unpaid governmental position—with the DC Public Defender Service. I got this internship—surprise, surprise—through my high school friend Amber. As I mentioned earlier, Amber's parents had started their careers in this office and had immense love for and loyalty to it.

The DC Public Defender Service, or PDS, had a very different vibe from that at the San Francisco Public Defender, which felt very DC versus California.

PDS had a prestigious reputation as one of the best public defender offices in the country. Unlike most public defender offices, PDS was federally funded, meaning we had new computers and central air-conditioning. The SF public defender was run-down, and we were always running out of pens.

At PDS, an air of superiority wafted through the halls with the chilly artificial breeze. Most of my co-interns were students at "HLS."

"What is this HLS I keep hearing about?" I asked Lara, who went to Berkeley with me. "Some local school?"

"It's Harvard, Anna," she said, seeming embarrassed I didn't know. "Harvard Law School."

News to me!

High-status public defender offices like PDS were strange places. Jobs there are nearly impossible to get despite the low pay—a starting salary of $60K versus roughly $200K at a Big Law firm. Public defenders are in court all day every day and are in trial all the time, which is a far cry from the document review that takes up most of the time of Big Law legal associates. Also, their offices are filled with geniuses, and these positions are often used as stepping-stones to higher-paid positions with the government or criminal defense firms. Their work is also *soooooo* much more interesting than the average law job. Instead of sifting through emails and contracts all day, public defenders whisk off to jails to interview defendants and argue before judges. Public defender work is filled with adrenaline that you wouldn't normally get at a Big Law firm, especially not in the day-to-day.

Despite the fact that we went to top ten law schools and demonstrated our commitment to criminal justice on our résumés, neither Amber nor I got a job at PDS following graduation from law school. Amber went on to work at a corporate law firm, where she makes a lot of money, but it was never her passion. She now has a kid and a mortgage and has left her dream of public defense behind completely.

This is what happens to a lot of lawyers: They start out wanting to make a change in the world, to be good lawyers and to serve justice, but either for financial reasons or simply because legal jobs in the public interest are really hard to get, they take a big-firm job, planning to work it for "just a few years." But then they become accustomed to a certain lifestyle. They have a child, get a mortgage. And then they're trapped in what has famously been called the golden handcuffs.

Amber didn't love her job in Big Law, but she was good at it. She had interned at the New Orleans Public Defender during her 1L summer, but for her 2L summer she took the OCI route and got a cushy job at a Big Law firm—the type of job I had been too inept to grab. (Roughly ten years later, she still works at that firm, despite numerous attempts to escape.)

Amber's parents helped me line up an internship in the appellate division of the DC PDS. I was better suited to appeals than trials.

Trials are for extroverts. They involve moving and chatting all day, running on adrenaline, thinking on your feet. I am not great on my feet. I don't like standing. I'm an introvert, and I need time to think. I felt much better doing research and writing alone than arguing before a judge or jury.

My preference for appeals was crystallized during the trial

practice class all PDS interns were required to take. We were given a mock case—an assault with a deadly weapon—and were tasked with crafting opening statements, direct examinations, cross-examinations, and closing statements.

The night before my mock cross-examination, I met Amber at a steamy DC bar.

"Think about me, Anna," Amber said, gripping the stem of her perspiring wineglass. She was excited, seemingly envious of my opportunity to participate in a mock trial at work. Working at a Big Law firm, Amber was spending her summer reviewing documents and schmoozing old white men. But trial was where Amber came alive. "Every single conversation I have is a cross-examination."

I laughed, but she wasn't really joking. I'd been friends with her since fourth grade and she could be really scary.

"Let's say Daniel flakes on me," she said, referring to her boyfriend. "I will confront him with a barrage of leading questions: *You texted me on Thursday at 2:04 p.m. that you were free on Saturday evening, correct? You said you would text me by Friday afternoon if things changed, right? And you did not text me on Friday afternoon, correct? I am therefore right to be upset that you canceled our plans on Saturday afternoon, isn't that fair to say?*"

I laughed. She had done this to me before.

I wasn't quite able to capture Amber's intensity during my own mock cross. My voice is naturally soft and unenthused and conveys a lot of uncertainty—I'm constantly changing my mind midsentence. I'm not very folksy or clear when I speak. And I'm not good at zeroing in on salient facts.

I'll never forget my supervisor's commentary after my mock direct.

"Anna," she said. "You asked a lot about the lighting, but you didn't ask a single question about the crime."

Sounds like me!

Luckily, the mock-trial class was only a few hours a week. The rest of the time I got to sit in my air-conditioned office, research cases, and Gchat with my friends.

I also got to participate in appellate division brainstorming sessions, which was cool because everyone was so smart. I would just sit there and be wowed by everyone's brains and chip in whenever the attorneys were confused about various slang terms, which I knew from listening to rap music.

My main assignment that summer involved suspected juror prejudice.

The facts were as follows. Kittle, a Black man, was charged with assault and related offenses. The jury found him not guilty of assault but could not reach a verdict on the related offenses. The trial judge declared a mistrial on the related offenses and dismissed the jury.

On the day the jury was dismissed, a juror sent a letter to the trial judge. In the letter, the juror said she enjoyed the jury experience but then stated:

> I strongly feel that this case should not have taken as long as it did with the deliberations but some of us were faced with dealing with some jurors feeling that all "blacks" are guilty regardless.

Defense counsel moved for a mistrial or, in the alternative, an investigation and evidentiary hearing into the allegations of racism. Pursuant to the "no impeachment rule," which holds that a juror is prohibited from testifying about deliberations after a verdict has been handed down, the judge denied the motion. The purpose behind the no impeachment rule is to promote verdict finality, encourage frank discussions in the jury room, and discourage postverdict harassment of jurors.

Given this rule, the issue of juror prejudice was tough to research. There weren't many cases on the subject. And the cases I could find were pretty horrifying. All day, I read about how juries had made decisions on the basis of race rather than law. A random cross section of the American public teems with implicit bias, which makes them very easy to emotionally manipulate, which is exactly what lawyers do. And in most of the cases I was reading, the appellate courts said the jurors' overt racism was fine!

Juror racism wasn't something I ever witnessed firsthand because jury deliberations are confidential and sealed, but I found memorable examples in the few relevant cases. Mostly instances of jurors assuming criminal defendants were guilty because they were Black or brown, as occurred in Kittle's case, or assuming civil defendants were guilty of chicanery because they were Jewish.

In a few cases, appellate courts agreed that inquiries into deliberations should be allowed in order to preserve the defendant's Sixth Amendment right to a fair trial. In particular, *United States v. Villar* (2009), where a juror said about a Hispanic defendant, "I guess we're profiling, but they cause all the trouble." In that case, the First Circuit held that the District Court could inquire into the validity of the verdict because the statement implicated the defendant's rights to due process and an impartial jury.

I wrote a memorandum citing this case and a few others.

My findings ended up in a brief that compelled the DC Court

of Appeals to announce a new rule of law. In *Kittle v. United States* (2013), the DCCA held that despite the general prohibition on juror impeachment, trial judges may consider juror testimony when claims of racial bias among jurors implicate the defendant's right to a fair trial. Specifically, the court held that trial judges can consider juror testimony in certain "rare and exceptional circumstances" when claims of racial or ethnic bias among jurors implicate the defendant's right to a trial by an impartial jury.

It sounds all nice and good, except the DCCA found no abuse of discretion in the trial judge's denial of the mistrial motion in Kittle's case. In other words, the juror's statement that some jurors felt that "all blacks are guilty regardless" was not the type of "rare and exceptional circumstance" that warranted an investigation.

If that statement didn't warrant the exception, I wasn't sure what would.

It hardly felt like a win.

This hardly-win prepared me for a career of similar experiences and planted the seeds of my cynicism. A juror said that "all blacks are guilty regardless" and the court said that horrifying statement didn't warrant a deeper look. And it wasn't some random redneck court in the Bible Belt that you might expect to casually endorse racism. It was the DC Court of Appeals— the appellate court of our nation's capital.

Law moves so slowly that I didn't even hear the news until my internship was long over and I was back at Berkeley in 3L year, more jaded than ever.

CHAPTER 7

Death Penalty Clinic

Law school flew by.

In 3L year, I joined the Death Penalty Clinic (DPC)—one of Berkeley's shining establishments. (In a law school clinic, students provide legal services to clients and gain hands-on experience.) I didn't really want to join, but extracurriculars were important and I was told it would be impossible to find a job after law school without them. Because I wanted to do postconviction criminal defense and the DPC did exactly that, my résumé would look weird if I didn't do it.

My internship in the appellate division of DC Public Defender Service didn't exactly make me want to race to an appellate criminal defense job. But it was the only type of law I could imagine doing. A law professor would have been my ideal legal career—reading books and writing papers and lecturing over-eager students on a beautiful campus with a cushy schedule—but I wasn't smart enough and didn't have the grades.

So appellate criminal defense was my next best bet.

I didn't want to do trials because, as I mentioned earlier, I can't think on my feet and don't like to stand on them either. I didn't want to work at a law firm because the fratty culture repulsed me and most of my cases would involve money, which I fundamentally do not understand.

Oh, also, no law firm would hire me.

Criminal defense is chock-full of human drama, and it involves philosophical questions about which acts society should punish and why. Criminal procedure is a challenging logic puzzle, enjoyable to nerds like me. It also involves fighting injustice, by holding corrupt cops and prosecutors accountable, the reason I went to law school in the first place. (Although I was feeling less and less optimistic about my ability to make a difference. . . .)

But I needed to do *something*. That was the real reason I went to law school: because I needed to do *something*. And it was the real reason I wanted to do postconviction criminal defense: because I needed to do *something*.

The DPC was led by a Didion-esque blonde named Camille who happened to be one of the top death penalty attorneys in the country. She had tired eyes and was super intimidating. Once she told us during a class on "managing stress to avoid alcoholism" that her biggest indulgence was waking up at five every morning to swim laps.

She was super scary and I admired her.

Camille made a point of taking on cases that no one else wanted because they were so grisly.

None of our clients were innocent. Some of them had killed kids. One client had killed a bride on her wedding day. Another client killed someone *on death row*.

These types of clients, Camille taught us, needed our help the most. Most postconviction criminal defense attorneys want to take on sympathetic clients—juveniles, victims of domestic abuse, clients they think might be innocent, clients who help them sleep at night. But Camille believed the unsympathetic clients needed more help because no one else wanted them. She didn't believe they were bad people and neither did I. They were people society had failed, people for whom, as she told us, "the notion of choice is artificial." She said this in reference to the "choice" to commit capital murder.

Despite the fact that our clients were of different ages and races and geographic locations, they all had experienced essentially identical childhoods. All of them were abused as children. They were all neglected. They were all dirt poor. They were all people of color. They were all diagnosed with PTSD and various other mental illnesses, which went back generations in their families.

After a while, I grew to see our clients more as victims than as perpetrators—despite their horrific acts. With what they had been through, and how society and their own families had deprived them, they didn't stand a chance of being functioning, law-abiding members of society.

My opposition to the death penalty isn't entirely moral. I do think some people are dangerous beyond rehabilitation and killing them is the safest and most efficient way to protect society. But those cases are very rare, and in practice the death penalty—as with most aspects of the criminal justice system—is used more as a vehicle of racism than anything else.

People of color have accounted for a disproportionate 43 percent of total executions since 1976 and compose 55 percent of those currently awaiting execution.[1] According to the Baldus Study—an analysis of race and the death penalty by law professor David C. Baldus and statistician George Woodworth—the odds of a death sentence being meted out are nearly four times higher if the defendant is Black.[2] The study also found that Black defendants convicted of killing white victims were more likely to receive the death penalty than any other racial combination of defendant and victim.[3]

But my main issue with the death penalty is what an epic waste of time and money it is.

In case you don't know (I didn't), the Supreme Court struck down the death penalty as unconstitutional in 1972. In *Furman v. Georgia*, a 5–4 majority held that the death penalty qualified as "cruel and unusual punishment" in violation of the Eighth Amendment. In particular, the court found states employed execution in "arbitrary and capricious ways," especially in regard to race.

But this holding wasn't a complete victory for death penalty abolitionists. The Supreme Court suggested new legislation that could make death sentences constitutional again, such as the development of standardized guidelines for juries.[4]

In the following four years, thirty-seven states enacted new death penalty laws aimed at overcoming the court's concerns about the arbitrary imposition of the death penalty. Several of these new statutes were upheld in 1976. In *Gregg v. Georgia*, the Supreme Court acknowledged progress had been made in jury guidelines and reinstated the death penalty under a "model of guided discretion."

In the meantime, death penalty statutes have become increasingly complicated in an effort to strike a compromise between conservative Law and Order types, who love punishment, and bleeding-heart liberals, who want to protect the due process rights of vulnerable populations.

As a result, death penalty litigation is *very* complicated.

On our first day in the Death Penalty Clinic, they taught us about the "nine boxes," or the nine opportunities a person convicted of a capital crime has to challenge his or her sentence.

Camille drew a lot of red arrows between boxes to show how the case could jump around.

What I grasped was that there were direct appeals and habeas petitions, and these were different, and there were procedures about how to get through both.

My crude understanding is that direct appeals happen first, and they're confined to using only the record created at trial. In other words, any information not included in the trial record is inadmissible in the appeal. On direct appeal, you argue that the judge made a wrong finding and that you should get a do-over. Habeas happens next, and it is not confined to the trial record. In habeas, you can introduce new facts. Like, say, someone came forward after a defendant was convicted and said he committed the crime—that is admissible in habeas, but not on direct appeal.

Following *Gregg*, when a person is charged with a capital crime, the state is constitutionally required to provide the defendant lawyers for life if the accused cannot pay for representation. Because of the way the criminal justice system operates in the United States, most capital defendants are poor and cannot pay for lawyers. This means that the state has to pay for lawyers for capital defendants to jump around between those nine boxes, *for life*. The state also has to pay for the prosecution.

This is very expensive!

According to a 2014 study, Pennsylvania spent $350 million

on the death penalty over a period during which the state executed just three people.[5]

How can executing three people possibly be worth hundreds of millions of dollars?

Our fucked-up death penalty scheme leads to all sorts of perverse results. For example, some murder defendants *want* the death penalty so that for life they get free lawyers, who also serve as therapists and companions because being in prison, I would imagine, is very fucking depressing. They also see themselves as having a better chance of getting out because of the nine boxes.

———

The clinic represented clients from jurisdictions all over the country, and we were split up into groups to assist the local attorneys. Some of our cases were at the trial level, some at the appellate, and some at postconviction.

My case was on remand—sent back—to the trial court, meaning box one of nine.

Amit, the new teaching fellow at the DPC, was my supervisor. He'd previously done death penalty work in New Orleans. My team was assigned to a nineties case from St. Charles Parish, Louisiana—a region in New Orleans. Our client, Ngai, was the one who had killed the bride on her wedding day. He was in love with her. He showed up at her wedding to another man and started an altercation. Then, he killed the father and the bride. He also shot but did not kill her mother, who escaped with her brother. Ultimately, he turned the gun on himself, shot himself, but survived.

The brother told authorities that he saw his sister's head "explode like a tomato."

The Louisiana Supreme Court had remanded the matter back to the trial court for an evidentiary hearing to address questions about whether subpar interpretation services were given to Ngai, who is Vietnamese, during his original trial. The interpreter had no training, spoke English poorly, and was not proficient in Vietnamese. Ngai spent significant portions of the trial with no understanding of what was happening, and his own testimony was mistranslated. Not that this was terribly surprising, given that the court had found the Vietnamese translator at a local laundromat. After an evidentiary hearing, the trial judge ordered that Ngai receive a new trial.

I didn't feel particularly invested in the case, mostly because it seemed so far away—geographically (the client and his primary legal team were two thousand miles away), temporally (the incident occurred in the nineties), and emotionally (the client didn't even know we existed). Also, Ngai murdered a family— a family that was very nice to him, that had helped him get on his feet when he immigrated to Louisiana from Vietnam—so it was hard to feel bad for him. And it was 3L year and, like I said, I was *slacking*.

Just four people made up Amit's team, and he split us up into groups of two.

My teammate, Clara, and I were tasked with making a chart documenting everything the jurors said during voir dire, which is just the elitist lawyer phrase for jury selection. We compiled this for a potential juror misconduct claim, which can include possibilities that the jurors were racist—as in the case I worked on during my PDS internship—or otherwise did not follow the

judge's instructions. If you are confused as to why we were researching juror misconduct when the case was on remand to the
trial court to determine whether the translator was ineffective,
join the club: I didn't get it either.

I suppose we were trying to get a sense of the jury pool
for potential future juror interviews, which is a typical part
of the habeas process. Given that habeas allows lawyers to
introduce new facts, it involves a lot of investigation, including
interviewing everyone who might have any information on
the crime, everyone who ever knew the defendant, and of
course the jurors, who might have inside information about
misconduct that occurred during deliberations, which could
give the defendant a chance to attack the procedure and get a
shot at relief.

But we were on remand to the trial court, so habeas was a
long way away, many boxes ahead.

In other words, we were preparing for a hypothetical future
situation that was not necessarily ever going to occur, and certainly not anytime soon. This added to the list of reasons it was
hard to be invested.

I honestly think Amit just couldn't think of anything else for
us to do.

The chart was supposed to take two weeks to create, and we
stretched it out to six months. No one seemed to care that we
took so long. We had given Amit this Enneagram personality
test that was all the rage in Berkeley. (The Enneagram is to
Berkeley as astrology is to Los Angeles.) Amit was a nine, or the
Peacemaker. This meant he was extremely conflict-averse and
would never call us out on anything. So we slacked and took
our sweet time on the juror chart.

(If you ever have a supervisor who is an Enneagram nine, consider yourself lucky and take advantage. And don't say you didn't get anything useful from this book!)

I believe Amit also didn't care that we took so long because it wasn't a pressing assignment. Death penalty litigation moves *very* slowly, and we were working on something that was relevant only to potential future litigation—way down the line on the nine boxes.

After spending six months on what was assigned as a two-week project, we were tasked with investigating the trial attorneys for potential misconduct.

This mostly involved googling the attorneys and trying to dig up dirt, which was fun as hell.

Much like the juror misconduct assignment, it was hard to see how doing this would have any impact whatsoever on our client, whose case was on remand to the trial court for the specific issue of the botched translation.

The Death Penalty Clinic was pitched to students as an opportunity to impact real clients, but obviously the most important work was completed by Ngai's primary litigation team in New Orleans. So we were tasked with very low-priority work, low down on the totem pole, the type of stuff attorneys give interns to keep them busy when they aren't really sure what to do with them.

In our boredom, Clara and I became convinced that the defense attorneys were sleeping together—without any evidence whatsoever (not very lawyerly).

We were particularly infatuated with the defense lawyer named Harper Boudreaux, a very New Orleans name. Harper had a blog at the time, which painted a very dark picture of her life—

lonely nights with a bottle of wine and her cat to help ward off the deep depression accumulated from years of representing murderers in a system that vindicated no one. "I specialized in death penalty trials for 11 years and it almost killed me," she wrote on her blog.[6]

Every week, we did *case rounds*, which involved meeting in a conference room and presenting updates in our cases to our fellow clinic members.

When it was Clara's and my turn to present, we channeled all of our creative energy into the presentation—which meant using Lindsay Lohan as a narrative thread. The troubled starlet was going through various legal battles at the time and there were loads of press images of her looking distressed in court-rooms, which I pasted all over our PowerPoint presentation. There was no connection between these Lindsay Lohan images and our case except that they both involved courtrooms; I just wanted it to look fun!

As the Peacemaker, Amit was okay with this.

During the presentation, we mostly talked about Harper Boudreaux, our theory that she was sleeping with her co-counsel, based on her blog and poetry.

I will never forget my classmates' blank faces when I read her haiku:

Barbwire barricades
Reek like bleach and boiled potatoes
Captive men wait to perish

The haiku was clearly about her clients on death row. It was all so dark.

Clara and I had addressed the cases with a journalistic fascination rather than a legal one. And the clinic was confused.

(To this day, I send this haiku to Clara every year on her birthday.)

Seven years after I graduated from law school, Amit emailed our DPC team. Attached to the email was the resentencing transcript from Ngai's case. After long negotiations, Amit explained, the team in New Orleans was able to persuade the DA to accept a twenty-five-year consecutive plea. He said the result came mostly from Ngai's expressions of remorse. This result, of course, had absolutely nothing to do with the work I did on the case.

But it was surreal hearing this news.

Our death penalty client not only was going to live but also was likely to be released from prison.

Our client who had killed the bride on her wedding day, her head exploding "like a tomato." Our client whom we'd never met, and who never knew we existed.

CHAPTER 8

By the end of law school, I was anxious about being a lawyer, about ending up like Harper Boudreaux, alone in my apartment chugging white wine and writing haunting haikus about men waiting to die. I was also starting to see the world, and how I sat in it, differently, particularly in the context of being a woman.

Growing up, I never considered myself a feminist. In fact, I had a negative association with the term. This partially came from my mom, a low-key men's rights activist, the type of woman who reads about a man being charged with rape and says, "As the mother of a son . . ."

("You have two daughters, you sick freak," I'd later hiss back at her.)

I'd internalized some of her attitude, I suppose. Feminists were weak. Frumpy. Stuck in the past. I wanted to live in the future. I also wanted to be pretty.

Plus, I didn't need to be a feminist. Even when I was in high school, it seemed glaringly obvious to me that women were superior to men. The women were better students and better at sports and generally got into better colleges. In college, all the smartest people I met were women. I just felt like female superiority was so apparent. What was there to fight for?

That changed the year before law school when I entered the San Francisco Public Defender, where the interns basically represented a meat market for the homicide attorneys. That's why Fernando told everyone I was a lesbian—to keep them away from me!

One day, Fernando approached the table where I worked and spoke to me in his whisper-yell.

"Anna, if you want to be taken seriously, you need to wear makeup," he said. "Your look is not professional."

I cowered, taken aback.

"Look at Leilani," he said. Leilani was a paralegal who wore pounds of foundation and hot-pink blush and thick eyeliner. She looked like a blow-up doll, or a drag queen. "You should be more like her."

I shrugged. "That's not really my vibe."

"Everyone loves Leilani," he said. His face lit up. "Today after work, I'm taking you to MAC."

I felt really conflicted: excited by the idea of him buying me makeup but also really hurt. No one had told me I needed to wear makeup before. I was convinced Fernando was calling me ugly.

After work, as promised, he put us in a taxi and took us to Pacific Heights—one of San Francisco's poshest neighborhoods and where Fernando lived. The taxi let us off right in front of the MAC store. Fernando strutted in and I shyly followed.

"I know you all don't do facial reconstructive surgery," he said to the shopgirls, waving around his American Express card. "But give this girl the next best thing."

The saleswomen and I shared an uncomfortable look.

"*Fernando,*" I squirmed.

"I'm kidding, I'm kidding," he said. "But really," he said, taking hold of one saleswoman's wrist, "give her a makeover and whatever makeup she needs to sustain it."

Fernando handed the woman his card and turned to leave. "I'll be getting a pedicure next door," he said. "Text me when you're done."

The woman sat me down in one of those elevated leather swivel chairs. "Sorry," I apologized sheepishly. "He's a lot." I'd grown used to apologizing for him.

"Seems like it," she said. "So, what is your current beauty routine?"

"I don't really have one," I said. "I splash water on my face sometimes."

I left MAC with $600 worth of makeup and an imaginary bill for thousands of dollars in future therapy for my fractured self-esteem.

Later, in law school, I told this story in my Feminist Jurisprudence class, when we were sharing stories about misogyny in the workplace. The angry feminists gasped, which felt partially justified and partially reductive. The story was complicated. It was about a battle within me, within all women, between the side of us that wants to be accepted and pretty, and the side that wants to buck the system and demand respect. I mean, the makeup was really nice and expensive. I still use it today. And Fernando's intentions were in the right place.

(And the fact that I'm still using makeup that was purchased over ten years ago and is likely expired proves Fernando's point that I probably needed some help in the beauty department.)

He wanted to do something nice for me.

It was still a struggle for me to find female role models in law school. My Feminist Jurisprudence teacher had shaggy gray hair and shopped exclusively in the "men's section of Eddie Bauer," she proudly announced early in the semester. Somehow, she was not a lesbian. The most popular female professors— like Nicole Porter—affected a masculine persona. They spoke algorithmically, wore suits designed to conceal the fact that they had female bodies, and haughtily referenced their clerkships with current SCOTUS justices every twelve seconds. They seemed to favor men, found nothing worth noticing in me, or any female classmate who didn't fit within their narrow vision of womanhood.

I didn't want to be anything like these women. The only professors I actually thought were cool were pointedly not professors. They were the legal writing instructors, also known as the "mommy instructors," because they all were women and most seemed to have kids. Everyone knew that they were paid the least, despite the fact that legal writing is by far the most relevant class to actually practicing law.

But in Feminist Jurisprudence, I was finally introduced to a legal scholar I admired: Catharine MacKinnon, the radical queen of feminist legal theory. MacKinnon—or "Kitty," as loved ones call her—has cold blue eyes, impeccable style, scathing opinions, and an iconic striped haircut that would make Susan Sontag jealous. Think of her as the Anna Wintour of the law. She is famous for her pioneering work in the areas of workplace sexual harassment and pornography laws, as well as for her incendiary public statements.

In 1975, while she was a law student at Yale, Kitty learned of an administrative assistant at Cornell who was refused a transfer when she complained about her supervisor's sexual advances. Then, when this administrative assistant resigned, she was denied employment benefits. Inspired by this account and others, Kitty began drafting her watershed book, *Sexual Harassment of Working Women*, which helped persuade the American judiciary that sexual harassment constituted a form of sex-based discrimination. Specifically, she argued that working women were sexually harassed *because they were women*, which made sexual harassment a form of gender-based discrimination.

Later, Kitty crusaded against pornography, calling it a civil rights violation. Along with her colleague Andrea Dworkin, Kitty argued that pornography should be actionable under the Fourteenth Amendment because of its explicit subordination of women, which in turn defines the treatment and status of half the population.

But it wasn't just her work I was taken with; I was equally interested in Kitty's public persona. As the *Chicago Tribune* put it in 1999: "During her 25 years in the public eye, Catharine MacKinnon has hardly been a stranger to controversy."[1] She's put herself at the center of a number of incendiary debates. She has argued rape laws are written to protect perpetrators rather than victims.[2] She was the first to convince the Supreme Court that sexual harassment constitutes discrimination on the basis of sex.[3] She's outspoken and ruthless and a convenient target for conservatives eager to dismiss feminism, who associate her with the quote "All sex is rape," even though she never said that. (But she has argued that all sex occurs within the context of gender inequality.)[4]

Back in 1993, Kitty seriously dated a "repentant womanizer" named Jeffrey Masson.[5] A psychoanalyst, Masson sued the *New Yorker* for $13 million after Janet Malcolm detailed his promiscuous past. Of note, he claimed to have slept with over a thousand women. Although their relationship didn't last, Masson apparently adored Kitty. As he told *New York* magazine: "She just sits and thinks deep thoughts. She is the greatest mind at work in the world today. . . . Hearing her lecture often makes me cry. I am immensely privileged to be living with her. It is like living with God!"[6]

Quelle romance!

After reading Kitty, I began to identify as a feminist. This doesn't mean I started protesting or anything. I didn't join any clubs or sign any petitions. I didn't buy any merch. But I started thinking about gender all the time.

I thought back to how I had made friends more easily with men in the beginning of law school. The men were less threatening because they didn't need to be threatening. They had taken a standardized test designed for them, scored well, and were entering a profession *for them by them*.[7] They didn't operate under the dual expectation to be competitive *and* friendly, high-achieving *and* put-together. They could be nice to people without worrying someone would read it as an invitation for sex—or worse—emotional labor.

Law school was always reminding us that men were superior. We were all tested on a case, which has since been overruled but which floats into my mind regularly, that deemed women "unfit" to practice law because of the "natural and proper timidity and delicacy which belongs to the female sex" (*Bradwell v. Illinois* [1873]).

One of my law school friends transitioned a few years after graduation. She therefore has had the unique experience of presenting both as a man and as a woman in legal settings. She said recently that a male supervisor told her she wasn't "aggressive enough"—something she'd never been accused of professionally when she presented as a man.

I wasn't shocked.

I'll never forget an experience I had in family court during my postgraduate clerkship, when I watched a woman fight for custody of her children. The woman was understandably emotional, crying and frazzled, as she tried to convey her points. Her ex-husband, by contrast, was cool and collected. He presented the way lawyers are trained to behave in a courtroom, the way judges respond to and respect: as if he's never experienced an emotion in his life.

The judge I was working with that day, a woman, called me into her chambers. "She's lying," she said about the woman, who'd painted a vivid picture of an abusive and absent father while begging for full custody of her children.

"Excuse me?" I asked.

"She's using those tears to manipulate me and I'm not falling for it," she said, before strutting back to the bench.

In law school, we aren't taught to understand people, their emotional experiences, or how structural inequality impacts their actions. Rather, we are taught to imagine the world in a vacuum, where everyone is rational and unemotional, and humans exist on a level playing field. *The reasonable man standard.*

Rufi Thorpe explains this phenomenon well in her 2020 novel, *The Knockout Queen*. It is unsurprising that the most accurate explanations of the criminal justice system I've read have come from novels, which capture the nuance of human darkness better than any logical, rule-based system can.

In one scene, the protagonist, Michael, sits in the courtroom awaiting his friend's arraignment. He has just watched a murder defendant, who was stood up by his lawyer, crying "against his will" in front of the judge. Michael observes:

> The judge did not have any tenderness or even any inclination toward civility for this young man. The fact that we would all be crying if our lawyer bailed on us during a hearing when we were accused of murder was not of consequence. . . . What was important to the judge was that the defendant maintain the decorum of the courtroom. That he controlled himself. Control was the matrix, was the soil, in which any kind of justice or rationality could grow, and if you did not carefully and rigorously maintain the atmosphere of control, then you would have no hope of clarity in anything.[8]

And of course, there is a gendered dimension to who maintains control.

Today, my female friends in Big Law complain that they are asked to do clerical work while their male counterparts litigate and draft contracts. They're expected to be the office caregivers and party planners, in addition to practicing law. They're paid less and expected to look better. Just imagine a female partner. She's impeccable. Not necessarily fashionable, but she's perfectly manicured—nary a snaggle in her tights or a frizz in her hair—and she's attentive and agreeable in social settings. Meanwhile, her male counterpart is sloppy and unkempt, telling the same self-aggrandizing story over and over again to whoever will listen.

I've often been called: mean, icy, a bitch. Looking back at my time in law, my resting cunt face was more of a defense mechanism than a snub. It was a way to avoid being sidetracked from my goals into needless emotional labor. I didn't have the energy to be a caretaker and a striver. Something had to give.

What I previously saw as character flaws unique to me were actually imposed on me, and all women, by the patriarchy. I spoke softly and without certainty because I'd been conditioned to be quiet and unsure of an opinion that didn't come from a man. In writing essays, I relied heavily on quotations for the same reason—I'd been taught to defer to the voices of others. I felt compelled to tell every single person that I was let into Berkeley off the waitlist because, like many other female achievers, I suffered imposter syndrome—meaning, I didn't think I *deserved* to be at such a prestigious institution.

In 3L, my last year in law school, I also started learning about my sexuality.

My boyfriend Charlie gave me a book for my birthday in 2L year called *How to Be More Confident*. I was livid. He was a nerdy white man who had gone to Harvard. He didn't understand the impossible standards high-achieving women were up against, how confidence could be misconstrued as bitchiness, how anything smart-sounding must be served with a side of self-deprecation to avoid alienating people.

"I'm not confident because I have received a lot of confusing messages!" I screamed.

It was convenient to simply attribute all my personality flaws to my gender, something random and completely out of my control. Although, in retrospect, I wonder whether I just wanted an out for being myself.

(In my teens, I thought *I* was the problem. In my twenties, I thought *society* was the problem. And in my thirties, I'm like, oh, yeah, no, *I'm* the problem.)

Charlie broke up with me second semester of 3L year, right after he got back from Birthright (the free trip to Israel offered to all young adults of Jewish descent). The breakup was awkward because in the weeks leading up to him leaving on his trip, I kept joking about him meeting a Jewish woman and breaking up with me. I mean, that's kind of the whole point of Birthright. But I never thought he would break up with me. That's why it was a joke!

But then he ended it with me just a few days after he returned.

I texted my mom: Charlie broke up with me.

She didn't respond. A few days later, on the phone, I asked her if she'd gotten my text. She said, "I did."

Well, I'm my mother's daughter.

My ego was a bit bruised, mostly because I thought I was better than him. But I wasn't too sad, just numb about it. Besides, I'd developed a new crush.

I had met Michael a month or so earlier at Bar Review. He was friends with Clara, my DPC teammate. When she introduced him to me, I was shocked that he was a law student: He had good style and seemed to know about culture. He wasn't bro-y or overconfident. He was shy and seemed sweet. But he had a quiet swagger. He was the opposite of Charlie, who was loud and abrasive in a way that made clear he was overcompensating for a major insecurity.

But as with Charlie, and every other boy I dated, I initially thought Michael was gay.

Michael and I became fast friends. He wanted to be a law professor, which I thought was hot, and we were both obsessed with A$AP Mob. He encouraged my creative side, which was refreshing after Charlie the Robot. We slept together not long after I told him that Charlie broke up with me, and the sex was surprisingly good. He was also really nice to me. He bought me a sketchbook and glitter paint pens. We would tag the parking lot across from my apartment late at night. I felt like Clover, the delinquent graffiti artist I had met through my roommates in San Francisco.

At one party, a very drunk girl I didn't care for cornered Michael and told him he was gay.

I stood there awkwardly, thinking, *Yeah, he's the gay one* . . .

No one saw it in me. The nice thing about being a woman was that I was completely invisible. Like, *I'm here, I'm queer, now watch me disappear.*

CHAPTER 9

Not Guilty by Reason of Insanity

Not long after I started seeing Michael, my classmate Justin went to Vegas, got drunk, stumbled into the wildlife habitat at the Flamingo Hotel, and ripped the head off a rare bird. A felony.[1]

One of my students when I was a legal writing TA, Eric, was his coconspirator. Eric was an introvert who dreamed of being a prosecutor, confirming what had been drilled into my head at public defender offices—that prosecutors are straight-up wicked.

Eric caught the buildup to the beheading on his iPhone camera, which law enforcement later used to secure an indictment. On the video, Eric repeats the phrase "we're going to be YouTube famous" as Justin chases the bird around the hotel's wildlife habitat while guests eat breakfast in the background. The video is cut short just before Justin catches the bird. The decapitation is not shown, which somehow makes it spookier.

"A witness then observed the suspects emerge from the trees," police said, "carrying the body and severed head of the bird."[2]

What makes his savage beheading of a harmless bird in broad

113

daylight all the more perplexing is the fact that Justin was an executive editor of *Ecology Law Quarterly*—Berkeley's environmental law review. He minored in environmental studies at UCLA and clerked for the Environment and Natural Resources Division of the DOJ.

I felt bad for the bird, an exotic helmeted guinea fowl who did nothing to deserve such a gruesome end. But my classmates' sympathy lay curiously elsewhere. "They'll never be able to practice law," the chorus echoed through the halls, as if that was the worst thing that could happen to someone.

Everything about 3L year was just . . . bizarre.

"Did you hear about Freya Freeman?" Spencer asked me one day as we were leaving Kelly's office.

"Who?" I asked.

"She's the director of the Center for Social Justice," Spencer said. "Apparently, she went loco at some event last night."

I didn't even realize we *had* a Center for Social Justice. I immediately went home and started googling. I recognized Freya's photo on our law school webpage. She had dreadlocks and small, round hipster glasses and looked much cooler than the average law school administrator. I'd noticed her around and had wondered if she was lost.

My Google search indicated that Freya had had a "public outburst" at a gala for prospective Black students. She told the students they would be in "danger" if they attended Berkeley Law and encouraged them to instead attend the "Justice School," a new law school she was originating.[3]

Saying you're going to found your own law school is definitely less crazy than decapitating a bird in broad daylight, but my classmates didn't see it that way. Apparently, my peers would rather rally around two Ozzy Osbourne–style bird killers than someone who, albeit a bit outlandishly, wanted to change the way law school was taught.

It was, of course, inappropriate for a school administrator to warn prospective students against attending the school she was paid to advertise. That said, I also understood where Freya was coming from. As a woman, I often felt like law school was a dangerous place. Maybe not literally (unless, of course, you are an exotic bird), but I certainly didn't feel safe to be myself. I cannot imagine being a queer person of color in an institution with such reverence for American history. Historically, the United States has been overwhelmingly hostile toward women, gays, and people of color. And law school is a place where we're taught to respect "precedent"—that is, the past.

The halls of Berkeley Law echoed with outrage. Freya Freeman was "crazy," "psychotic." There was no sympathy for Freya like there was for the boys who had decapitated the innocent bird. Instead, the student body seemed to agree Freya was evil to betray their beloved law school.

After she lost her job, Freya sued Berkeley. The named defendant was her former supervisor, Maribelle Cromwell. Freya claimed her boss did not find her "sufficiently appreciative" of Cromwell's "self-perception as a 'White Savior' of 'people of color.'"

Although students laughed at this language, it did not seem out of left field to me. White savior complexes ran rampant at Berkeley Law; the institution was filled with blonde women screaming about racial injustice.

I was one of them!

These days, most white women are performatively woke—just

scroll through your social media feed for thirteen seconds. But that wasn't the norm in 2011, although it was standard practice at Berkeley Law, perhaps a vestige of Berkeley's revolutionary spirit in the seventies.

But watching my classmates turn against Freya for her legitimate breakdown—one clearly born of racial injustice—showed me just how empty their wokeness was.

Freya wasn't the only faculty member to "go crazy" at Berkeley Law.

After I graduated, I heard that my favorite writing instructor, Rhonda, was let go on dramatic terms. Rhonda taught Advanced Legal Writing in my 2L year.

I missed the first class, and Spencer G-chatted me: "You're going to *love* the instructor. She kinda reminds me of Lisa Love from *The Hills*."

(I had to google the reference. *The Hills* never did it for me. If I wanted to watch a bunch of vacant blondes with too much money and nothing to say, I'd go back to high school.)

But Spencer was right about the first part. I loved Rhonda instantly.

First, there was her polyester tracksuit, a sharp departure from the boxy suits most law professors wore. Next was the two-liter bottle of Diet Coke that never left her grip. Best of all was her attitude, which I think is where the Lisa Love comparison came in. Rhonda was scathing and nihilistic. She would mock overeager students to their faces and talk openly about her depression in the manner of a social media–addicted millennial.

She didn't shy away from controversy. Two weeks after the aforementioned bird decapitation story hit the halls, she strutted into class and unfolded a massive newspaper to a photo of the perpetrators and said, "Let's discuss." She didn't have a "take," per se, she just wanted to hear what we thought. Which was, like, unheard of in law school. No one cared what we thought. Professors typically only cared what the Supreme Court thought.

Her kooky irreverence was so . . . refreshing!

From her frequent monologues about herself at the beginning of class—much like a late-night host—it seemed Rhonda's life had taken a downward turn in the past decade or so. After graduating from law school, she became a successful employment law attorney in Chicago and then San Francisco. She left Big Law to direct Berkeley's First-Year Skills Program but was gradually demoted over the years, I assumed because of her, well, quirky personality and her utter inability to play the game. At this point, she taught only one class—Advanced Legal Writing, which hardly anyone took. (It wasn't tested on the bar.)

There were five students in our class, two of whom were named Brad. Rhonda quickly nicknamed them "Good Brad" and "Bad Brad," I don't remember why. But she had a very obvious crush on Bad Brad, evidenced by how she frequently used his name in case examples and giggled whenever she did it. Leave it to Rhonda to prefer the "bad" one in the dynamic she'd invented for herself. Truth be told, it was kind of metal.

Spencer and I quickly developed a friendship with Rhonda. We would stay after class and chat with her, pretending to have questions about the assignments, just to hear her peculiar opinions on things. She told us she was writing a novel "about mental illness" and talked a lot about her childhood friend, who also was named Rhonda.

She said people called her "Big Rhonda" and her friend "Little Rhonda" to keep them straight, sort of like Good Brad and Bad Brad. Little Rhonda and Big Rhonda were always getting into petty fights over nothing, which I loved hearing about. Listening to her talk reminded me of watching *Real Housewives*. I felt that way with a lot of my legal writing teachers. Most of them were married to rich men, didn't work long hours, lived lush lives, and had big personalities. Rhonda's life didn't appear lush, but she made up for it with her offbeat charm.

One evening, Spencer and I convinced Rhonda to go for drinks with us at a bar across the street from the law school. We sat drinking and chatting for about three hours. Toward the end, I tried to get Rhonda to smoke weed with me.

She said she would, but not that night.

Not long after, Rhonda tried to set me up with Bad Brad in a transparent effort to live vicariously through me, as he was strictly off-limits to her. In a detailed email structured much like a bench memo, she told me I had "three options."

1. you're not interested (I already have a backup for this scenario—so you won't hurt his feelings). but you should tell me so i don't keep talking you up.

2. you're interested enough so he could call and ask you out.

or 3. you like him but need to get to know him better, which i guess means you and spencer ask him out together, etc.

here's what he said about you, anna: she's pretty and nice and smart (I'm not sure in what order he said them), so of course he thinks she's probably just too good for him.

I'm not sure how you can resist that, but I did tell him you had some kind of quasi-boyfriend so I'd find out whether you were interested.

I responded that given my "quasi-boyfriend"—Michael—I probably shouldn't date Bad Brad. She seemed relieved. "I take it you are fine if I set him up with someone else?" she responded. "I mean I earmarked him for you and all, but if you have too many suitors, I ran into a former student and thought that was a possibility."

It was all so inappropriate; I loved it! Rhonda was such a delicious break from all the rigid propriety of law school.

I liked how open she was about sexuality. She wrote her memo like I had all the power in whether I wanted Bad Brad or not. I was still trying to understand my growing feelings toward women. But I wouldn't tell her that. I hadn't learned to prioritize my own desire, or even consider it at all. Growing up, my friends and I didn't talk about masturbating or porn or having orgasms the way boys do. The goal of sex, I was taught, was the male orgasm. I didn't initiate sex; I drank myself into submission. Who cared what would make me feel good? I didn't have the power, he did. I got off on starving myself instead: literally, figuratively, emotionally. As a woman, I'd been taught, my goal was to be as small as possible. To be invisible. To make myself disappear.

In middle school, the word *slut* was thrown around a lot as an insult. In college, I finally took a stand against it; I made a vow that I would not give a man a blow job unless he at least offered to go down on me first. I did not, and do not, even particularly like being eaten out. But it was a matter of principle, a protest against the unjust glorification of the male orgasm. This was as close as I ever got to being an activist. Today, I see withholding my perfect spinner body from the male gender as the political act of a lifetime! I don't need to go to a protest. My *existence* is a protest.

I definitely took out my newfound feminism on my boyfriend. We were having sex less, and I felt it was important to call out his entitlement at every chance I got, the bigger the audience the better. When he complained about traffic while driving a group of our friends to San Francisco on the weekends, I'd say: "I know you're used to the world catering to your every desire, but these roads are for everyone, and the other drivers have as much of a right to be here as you do." I'd make intense eye contact through the rearview mirror. "The road is not for you alone." It was the Rhonda in me.

Aside from her lust for Bad Brad, the only thing that seemed to make Rhonda happy was her favorite case, *Smith v. Midland Brake, Inc.*, 180 F.3d 1154 (10th Cir. 1999)—affectionately, *Midland Brake*.

I never understood why Rhonda was so obsessed with *Midland Brake*, a convoluted nineties Tenth Circuit case about the Americans with Disabilities Act (ADA). *Midland Brake* holds that if an employee with disabilities can be accommodated by reassignment to a vacant position, the employer must do more than merely consider that employee alongside other applicants. Instead, the employer must actively offer the employee with disabilities the vacant position. But as with most legal principles, there are, like, a thousand exceptions. The case is confusing. And obviously not particularly interesting.

But Rhonda talked about it constantly and had a revelation about it almost every day. She'd storm into class and regale us on how she realized a certain sentence meant something different from what she previously thought it did. *Midland Brake* was this rich, ever-shifting source of wisdom to her. Like a well of truth, her spiritual guru, her Bible.

I wondered whether Rhonda had, at one point in her career, been denied reasonable accommodation pursuant to the ADA. Otherwise, I could not understand why she was so obsessed. It seemed very personal to her.

Unsurprisingly, our big assignment that semester was a bench memo about the Americans with Disabilities Act that would necessarily rely on *Midland Brake*.

The fake case was called *LeBlanc v. Sunshine Foods, Inc.* The plaintiff was an employee with a disability who claimed his former employer, the defendant, failed to accommodate him under the ADA. The defendant moved for summary judgment— a judgment entered based on the undisputed facts, without a full trial.

The legal issue concerned the appropriate rule to apply when the ADA's duty to reassign an employee with disabilities to a vacant position conflicted with an employer's policy to hire the "most-qualified applicant" for a vacant job. There was no authority in the Eleventh Circuit, the circuit we were pretending to write from, and a split of authority in the other circuits.

In my "brief answer," which was not particularly brief, I explained that given the Supreme Court's majority opinion in *U.S. Airways, Inc. v. Barnett*, the fictional court would likely find that reassignment in contravention of Sunshine's most-qualified-applicant policy was reasonable "in the run of cases" under the ADA.

I reasoned that Mr. LeBlanc's requested reassignment was not in violation of a seniority policy, and reassignment to a vacant position was otherwise presumed reasonable. Even if the fictional court should find that reassignment was not ordinarily reasonable, it would likely find that special circumstances existed—namely, that Sunshine could unilaterally change its policy and had done so twice in four years, and that the formalized policy affected relatively few employees—which made reassignment reasonable under the particular facts of our case. However, additional facts needed to be developed to determine whether Sunshine could rebut the reasonableness of the reassignment with a showing of undue hardship. Either way, I concluded, Mr. LeBlanc had likely offered sufficient evidence to defeat Sunshine's motion for summary judgment.

Boring, I know!

But I loved using my perpetual confusion about the circuit split as an excuse to visit Rhonda's office hours and listen to her monologue about various random subjects.

I tried to keep in touch with Rhonda after her class ended that year, which wasn't easy. It was hard enough to reach her when she was my teacher, but when she wasn't, it was like trying to get in touch with Madonna.

When I visited the Bay Area the year after I graduated, I emailed Rhonda to get drinks.

She didn't respond for three months—long after I'd returned to DC. "I was not ignoring you! I only do that to current students!" she wrote back. Then she told me the Berkeley Law "email-merger computer guy" told her what she had "long suspected"—that she "didn't exist on the system." She concluded: "I first thought I was fired, then I figured it was all for the best, because I don't really want to read email anyway."

If this were fiction, we would call that second-to-last line *foreshadowing*.

Rhonda also told me that Michael, the boy I'd been "quasi-dating" when she tried to set me up with Bad Brad, was her favorite student that semester. I reached out to him afterward and showed him Rhonda's email.

"Haha I love how she has the same excuse for everything," he said. "Like, bitch, just admit you ignore email. Don't tell me some story about how your email account 'doesn't exist.'"

I laughed, then asked, "Has she done that to you?"

"She told us that in class, like, every day," he said. "I'm going to forward you this email she sent us one time when she canceled class."

Subject: NO CLASS TODAY 11/13

Group: Site

Message:

Hi all—

I am reluctantly canceling class today. I am not feeling well.

I told some of you I recently finished a 6-month course of

Accutane; the side effects are still lingering—I think I ripped
something in my hip and burned a hole in my stomach as
well. The pain meds I took have not worked well enough—so
I don't think I can make it in. (My skin, however looks great! I
feel I am routinely mistaken for someone in their early to mid
thirties, so it was all worth it in the end!)

Toward the end of 3L year, I heard from Kelly, the program
director, that Rhonda had been assigned to teach 1Ls the next
semester.

She sensed impending disaster. So did I.

I knew from TA'ing 1Ls that they needed to be coddled.
Early in my TA experience, an anxious student had cornered
me in the hallway after class with tears streaming down her
face, desperately seeking confirmation that she was not, in fact,
stupid. (Everyone in law school had a deep-seated fear that they
were stupid, and I was no exception.) My job was equal parts
instructor and therapist. I wasn't great at this, but Rhonda was
worse. In addition to openly mocking students to their faces, she
was also wildly unpredictable, constantly modifying assignments,
and always responding to inquiries weeks late if at all.

Rhonda was teaching 1Ls after I graduated, and I asked her to
write a recommendation when I was applying for an MFA. She
always seemed to like my writing and was working on a book
herself (her mental illness novel). Also, she seemed to be the only
person I met in law school equipped to write a recommendation
for a creative program. In other words, she wasn't left-brained to
a fault. She had artistic sensibilities. This is why I liked her.

During our email exchange about the application process,
she wrote:

> This week a few of my mean girl students went to the dean
> of students to say I'm incompetent and ask to be moved to
> another section of 1L LRW! these kids are so oblivious to the
> world they really have no idea who is their friend and who is
> their enemy.

This email worried me. From my perspective, Rhonda was already on shaky emotional ground. Mentally stable people, in my understanding, brush their hair and don't guzzle Diet Coke like it's water. This email suggested she was reaching some kind of breaking point.

Soon after, Kelly told me Rhonda had been let go. Kelly was vague, and I was dying for details.

When I moved back to Oakland after my DC clerkship following graduation, I somehow convinced Rhonda to meet me for coffee. I was shocked when she showed up. She was wearing her typical tracksuit and immediately announced that she didn't drink coffee.

"They don't have Diet Coke here," she said, "so I'm going to get a beer."

It was eleven a.m.

We sat outside in the sun with our Sierra Nevada and coffee and chatted for three hours.

Rhonda told me she had to give up her San Francisco apartment after losing her job at Berkeley. She claimed the administration had been trying to oust her for decades, which I partially believed but which also sounded vaguely paranoid, and that they gave her 1Ls as a strategic move to push her over the edge. She was living with her sister in a remote suburb and working on her novel.

She hadn't spoken to Bad Brad.

That afternoon was the last time I spoke with Rhonda. Since then, she hasn't responded to any of my emails, and there have been many.

After my five-year reunion—I didn't go—Spencer told me that he got coffee with Kelly. According to Kelly, Rhonda had recently shown up to the law school in the midst of some sort of episode. She was claiming another legal writing professor was a nurse who was trying to institutionalize her.

It all felt very sad.

A 2011 *Psychology Today* article on the high rate of mental illness among lawyers declares: "Unfortunately, the stigma and secrecy surrounding mental illness often preempts impaired lawyers from seeking help until it is too late."[4]

CHAPTER 10

The Bar

Before I knew it, it was time to study for the California Bar Exam. We took the bar the summer after graduation, which was a boring blur, and before our first legal jobs, which would be a boring blur.

Like most aspects of law school, I didn't really understand what I was getting into until it was happening. Emily and Spencer signed up for the prep class BARBRI, which was a hybrid of Bay Area Review (BAR) and Bar Review Inc. (BRI), two companies that had merged in the seventies. Most of my classmates also signed up, so I signed up, too. The class met several times a week for three to five hours. Then we had practice tests and *lots* of homework.

Confession: I loved it.

Sure, I hated certain sections—Business Associations and Property Law were the worst. But I loved all the tests. Nothing quite gets your mind off your mundane insecurities and the looming fear of the unknown like a concrete set of complex problems you're granted a score for solving. I loved competing with myself in the sleek air-conditioned library. I loved my study group, which consisted of my friend Lara and her friend, this beautiful boy from Hastings with the most mesmerizing blue eyes. (Both Emily and Spencer were taking the New York State Bar, so we couldn't study together.) I loved listening to Blue Eyes explain mortgages to me.

I loved taking breaks to go running around Berkeley while listening to *Yeezus*, which dropped that summer and remains one of my favorite albums of the decade . . . maybe ever.

I often credit Kanye with my passing the bar. I wonder if his wife, Kim Kardashian, will do the same when she inevitably passes the bar.

I loved the adrenaline of having to master thirteen subjects in three months, many of which I was encountering for the very first time, like Business Associations, a section that tests things like partnership formation, agency, and vicarious liability.

Early in the summer, a group of us went to Lake Tahoe for our last hurrah before the bar. Law school was full of last hurrahs—day trips to Napa and weekends in Big Sur, drinking binges in anticipation of our impending indentured servitude to the law.

Drunk in our cabin one night, Spencer shouted: "Lesbian by estoppel." I don't remember what inspired it, but we clung to the term, and began riffing. Lesbian by estoppel, we joked, can be invoked when a woman claims a man sexually assaulted her. If the alleged assault survivor can produce sufficient prima facie evidence of lesbian tendencies, there arises a rebuttable presumption of lesbianism. Such evidence can include: (1) more than one pair of cargo shorts; (2) a Home Depot gift card; and (3) beyond de minimis welding or roller-derby experience. If the accuser cannot rebut this presumption, he is estopped from claiming that the woman acted in a heterosexual manner.

Later, back in Berkeley, Spencer and I kept the bit going. In between practice tests, Spencer was G-chatting with a friend who was studying for the bar in Texas. Spencer was literally *always* on Gchat, and I was on it almost as much as he was. (When I wasn't, I was likely drinking.)

"Have you figured out lesbian by estoppel?" Spencer G-chatted his friend.

"I've never heard of it," she responded quickly, her panic seemingly emanating from the screen. It's very cruel to take advantage of someone's anxiety during bar prep, but we were *so bored.* Spencer went along with it for hours, while I watched, explaining that the doctrine was likely prominent in Texas, because it was "based on outdated assumptions about gender and sexuality."

I cackled.

The next day—I believe it was Derivative Suit Day at BARBRI—we created a Google Doc to define the term, which we eventually expanded into a larger document entitled "Essential Principles of Lesbian Law," alternatively, "The Vagna Carta." We defined the terms in outline form, the format we used to study for exams and the bar. There are twenty-six terms in total.

What can I say? We were creatively stifled. The Vagna Carta came from the same impulse as the Lindsay Lohan PowerPoint: a desperate need to lighten the mood.

Also, perhaps I was expressing some repressed lesbian desires. Perhaps!

At that time, the California Bar Exam included three full days of testing, six hours each day. (They've since changed it to two days.) Studying involved three or four hours of BARBRI class a day, then five or six hours of homework. It was like a full-time job. It sounds crazy to study full-time for a test for three months, but it's not so crazy when you consider the breadth of material.

The test consisted of three portions. First was the Multistate Bar Examination (MBE), a six-hour examination containing two hundred multiple-choice questions. The MBE tests seven subjects: Civil Procedure, Constitutional Law, Contracts, Criminal Law and Procedure, Evidence, Real Property, and Torts.

Then there was the performance test, which was intended to mimic a real-life legal task, like writing a legal memo or drafting an affidavit. The performance test is no longer part of the California Bar, and as far as I remember, we didn't study for it.

Finally, there was the General Bar Exam, the portion that is unique to California. It tests the following thirteen subjects:

- Business Associations
- Civil Procedure
- Community Property
- Constitutional Law
- Contracts
- Criminal Law and Procedure
- Evidence
- Professional Responsibility
- Real Property
- Remedies
- Torts
- Trusts
- Wills and Succession

On the actual exam, you're only tested on a few of these subjects. But you don't know which, so you have to prepare for all thirteen. In a whole universe of YouTube videos, "experts" predict which subjects will be tested on the next California Bar Exam, sort of like how meteorologists predict the weather.

Lara, Blue Eyes, and I would study in the Death Penalty Clinic office on the fifth floor of the law school. The room was stuffy and had no AC, which was unfortunate because it was a hot summer, and for those who haven't spent time in the region, the East Bay, where Berkeley is located, is significantly hotter than chilly San Francisco.

But on the plus side, the room had killer views of the bay. And it required a code to get in, which Lara and I had from our stint in the clinic, so we normally had the room to ourselves, meaning we could avoid our classmates' frantic energy.

The bar made everyone really anxious, which made studying with Lara nice—she was very unbothered by it all. She told me she was a naturally good test taker. She spent most of the summer having sex and working out.

In bar class, Lara would be glued to the Instagram explore page on her phone, mostly looking at fitspo—in particular, butts she found aspirational. She would tap my shoulder during lectures to show me rock-hard derrières, which aren't really my taste, but I would pretend to be impressed for the sake of friendship.

In our study sessions, Lara would sprawl out on the couch in the corner and message guys on OkCupid.

A few weeks before the test, Lara came into the study room giddy. She was often giddy during our study sessions, but this time it was about neither a boy nor a butt.

"Come here," Lara announced, propping up her laptop on a table.

Blue Eyes and I gathered around the screen.

Lara pulled up a PDF. It was a page of predictions from someone named "Professor Heilman."

"This guy is supposed to be the best," she said. "He apparently always gets it right. And we can just study for these subjects."

We all read the document in a state of rapture.

Heilman claimed his predictions were "educated guesses" based on reviewing the bar exam for more than twenty-five years. He said that he was typically correct on anywhere from two and a half to six questions. He said that he had correctly predicted four of the six total essay questions on the General Bar Exam portion of the most recent exam. He explained that the general portion of the California Bar Exam typically tested two to four multistate subjects and at least one subject that addressed California law specifically, like Community Property, and that Professional Responsibility would be tested in some fashion on every single exam. Professor Heilman suggested that we study every subject because overall the exam was unpredictable, which I assumed he stated to avoid getting sued by resentful and litigious law grads.

Then he gave his predictions on which subjects would be on this year's exam using a scale from *more likely* to *possible* to *less likely*.

I decided to focus my studying on the *most likely*, and I did not study the *less likely* subjects.

To my absolute delight, Business Associations was a *less likely* subject. For this reason, I trusted Heilman. Not because I understood statistics and trusted his methodology, but because I desperately wanted it to be true. No matter what, I just couldn't wrap my head around shareholder derivative suits. Or really anything else involving "money."

Lara *exclusively* studied the *most likely* subjects. She started listening to the BARBRI lectures online on 4× speed. She listened to them all in the week before the test, sitting in the corner of the study room with a sort of crazed look in her eyes, like she was some kind of mad genius.

She also slept with Blue Eyes that week.

Michael dumped me a few weeks before the test. He seemed shocked that I didn't protest when he brought up the idea of cutting romantic ties. He was really just a rebound, which is rude to admit, but true. I never thought I would marry the guy. He was sweet, but I wasn't attached. This of course might have had something to do with the fact that he was a man.

"I don't want you to fail the bar because of me," he said.

I laughed and hung up.

I was busy in bar land anyway. My apartment had started to look like the jail cell in *A Beautiful Mind*. Handwritten outlines and cryptic notes were stuck all over my walls. I studied all day every day and spent the evenings pacing around my apartment and reciting strings of words I'd memorized to earn easy points on the essays.

The Uniform Commercial Code (UCC) applies to all contracts with respect to the sale of goods.

The statute of limitations serves as an absolute bar to legal action.

California is a community property state, and there is a presumption that property acquired during the marriage is community property.

Since I was smoking weed less to study, my brain felt sharper than ever. But I wasn't any less paranoid. I was having recurring and intrusive thoughts about getting in a car accident on the way to the exam.

I guess for this reason, a lot of people rent a room in the

hotel where the test is administered, which was at a Marriott in downtown Oakland. But that sounded too scary to me, being around all that anxious and desperate energy.

———————

The day before the test, I loaded my phone with rap music that made me feel confident—Kanye West and Nicki Minaj and Lil Wayne—and set my alarm for seven a.m.

The Marriott was about a fifteen-minute drive from my apartment in Berkeley. I left thirty minutes before testing started, leaving time for traffic but minimizing time lingering around all that nervous energy in the lobby. On the drive, I yelled, "I'd rather be a dick than a swallower" along with Kanye and felt ready for battle.

Entering the lobby, a tidal wave of nerves—not just my own but others'—hit me. I tried to keep my distance, but the people around me vibrated with a stress frequency so damn loud, shouting about how this was their third or fourth or even seventh time taking the test.

"Seventh time's a charm!" yelled a girl with a rollie backpack to no one in particular.

I felt dizzy.

I made a vow to myself right then and there that if I didn't pass, I would find a new profession. There was no way in *hell* I was doing this again. To this day, I still have nightmares about having to retake the bar exam. This was the kind of experience I had the emotional energy to do only once, maybe like moms who stop after just one kid.

We weren't allowed to eat or drink in the testing room, which was massive and filled with probably fifty rows of desks. According to the State Bar of California, only the following items are allowed in the examination room without prior approval:

- The admittance ticket with no writing on it
- Nondigital pens (if you are handwriting the examination, you must bring your own pens with blue or black ink)
- Pencils (mechanical pencils are not allowed)
- Silent analog watches, nondigital timers, and clocks measuring four inches by four inches or smaller
- Rulers
- Paperclips
- Pen-style highlighters (must not be used on answers)
- Inhalers
- Disability-related items that have been approved through the testing accommodations petition process
- Cash (must not have writing on it), credit/debit cards that might be needed for the lunch break (wallets may not be brought into the test center)
- Eyeglasses (no cases or sunglasses)
- Foam earplugs (must not be connected)
- Feminine hygiene items
- Prescription medication
- Diabetes-related equipment (does not include food or drinks)
- Eyedrops in single-use vials
- Government-issued photo ID
- Keys
- Back support
- An orthopedic cushion
- A standard-size pillow without a case

- One bookstand
- One footrest
- Splints and braces
- Crutches
- Wheelchairs
- Casts
- Hearing aids
- TENS units
- Laptop accessories: separate keyboard, mouse (wired or wireless), laptop riser/stand no higher than four inches, and solid color mouse pad with no writing on it (written sessions only)[1]

The list alone nearly sent me into cardiac arrest.

I never did understand what the rulers were for—dick measuring?

During the MBE sessions, or the multistate multiple-choice portion of the exam, the items listed above were allowed in the examination room . . . except for pens, rulers, paperclips, highlighters, back supports, orthopedic cushions, pillows, bookstands, and footrests.

There were also detailed instructions regarding writing instruments: "Several sharpened pencils are recommended; mechanical pencils are not permitted."[2]

I thought these rules were bad, but Amber was taking the bar in Virginia—and test takers were required to wear a full suit to the exam. According to the Virginia Bar website, while "the Board is aware that many law firms and other professional offices have 'dress down' policies of varying descriptions" there "is no 'dress down' or 'casual dress' policy at the Virginia Bar Exam."[3]

Ruthless!

The website goes on to explain "appropriate attire," which for men includes a "coat and tie" and for women includes a "dress, suit, or pantsuit."

It gets more insane. "Due to the nature of the floors at the testing site" (?????), and "as a courtesy to other applicants" (?????), "court-appropriate soft- or rubber-soled shoes are preferred."

My favorite is the last line: "Recognizing the high caliber of professionalism that has traditionally characterized the bar, the Board is confident that no further discussion of this topic will be necessary."

Savage!

Amber told me she saw someone get kicked out because she was wearing the wrong type of shoes, which—to Amber—looked perfectly "court-appropriate." At San Francisco Superior Court, lawyers wore Nikes and stripper heels, so I wasn't sure what this directive meant exactly. It seemed the shoe standard was relative.

Day 1 was the Multistate Bar Examination. And it was a hot mess. It felt like 80 percent of the questions were about mortgages, the subject that I wanted to avoid the most and that, apparently, Blue Eyes hadn't done a very good job of explaining. Actually, it wasn't his fault. It was mine. I was stupid, like I'd always known. I did not remotely understand the questions. For your reference:

---

8. A woman borrowed $800,000 from a bank and gave the bank a note for that amount secured by a mortgage on her farm.

Several years later, at a time when the woman still owed the bank $750,000 on the mortgage loan, she sold the farm to a man for $900,000. The man paid the woman $150,000 in cash and specifically assumed the mortgage note. The bank received notice of this transaction and elected not to exercise the optional due-on-sale clause in the mortgage. Without informing the man, the bank later released the woman from any further personal liability on the note.

After he had owned the farm for a number of years, the man defaulted on the loan. The bank properly accelerated the loan, and the farm was eventually sold at a foreclosure sale for $500,000. Because there was still $600,000 owing on the note, the bank sued the man for the $100,000 deficiency.

Is the man liable to the bank for the deficiency?

(A) No, because the woman would have still been primarily liable for payment, but the bank had released her from personal liability.

(B) No, because the bank's release of the woman from personal liability also released the man.

(C) Yes, because the bank's release of the woman constituted a clogging of the equity of redemption.

> (D) Yes, because the man's personal liability on the note was not affected by the bank's release of the woman.

Now imagine answering over one hundred questions like that in a room filled with people basically hyperventilating.

I know.

I think you had to get only around 50 percent correct to pass, but in the moment I didn't see how I could possibly do that.

Day 2, the performance test, was somehow even worse. It was a very complex business question, a language I don't understand. Reading it made me dizzy. And as I looked at the clock halfway through the allotted three hours, I realized I still had no idea what the question was even asking.

I just started typing.

I didn't really know what I was saying. I was just typing vague strings of words that sounded both business-y and lawyerly, like "fiduciary duties," "piercing the corporate veil," "preemptive rights," and "quorum."

At one point I looked up and saw someone in front of me being removed from the testing room. He was surrounded by administrators speaking in hushed tones. I wasn't sure if he was cheating or had the wrong type of pencil or what. I wanted to snoop, but I didn't have time! I just kept typing, typing and typing and typing, and eventually time was up.

Everyone was panicked as we left the exam room, which made me feel a little better.

Even Charlie the genius was freaking out. *What the FUCK*

was that??? What the FUCK!!! I sort of enjoyed watching him squirm.

Day 3 was better, which isn't saying much given how abysmal the first two days had been.

I really lucked out with the essays. There were no Business Associations questions, thank God.

They tested us on Torts, Community Property, Wills and Trusts, and Constitutional Law. Torts is really easy. I still remember: *duty, breach, causation, damages.* Community Property is about dividing marital assets on the basis of a simple set of rules. Wills and Trusts is also fairly straightforward. Also, I'd gotten Honors in the class. And Con Law is just fun. Con Law is what most people think of when they think of law school. Civil rights and such.

I don't believe in God, necessarily, but if I did, I would say she was on my side that day. Or maybe it wasn't God. Maybe it was *Yeezus.*

———

The results weren't released until months later, around late November, when I had already moved back East. They went up online on Friday night.

I felt physically ill all week, but Friday was torture. I felt like I was going to faint all day. It wasn't that I wanted to be a lawyer. It was that I needed to pass the bar, or else it would reveal something horrid about me. It would mean my imposter syndrome wasn't a syndrome after all. It would mean that I *was* an imposter. It would mean Berkeley let me in exclusively because it needed to fill the class and knew I could pay, or, rather, my granny could pay. It would invalidate every academic accomplishment I'd ever achieved in my entire life. Phi Beta Kappa? Latin nonsense. My 3.94 GPA in college? It was a state school. My 168 on the LSAT? Whatever. My acceptances into UVA, Berkeley, USC, and UCLA Law? Meaningless.

Nothing I'd ever done would matter if I didn't pass the bar.

That Friday after work, I sat on my childhood bed with my laptop—I was living at home at the time—and just kept refreshing the website.

Before the list came up on my computer, a text came in from Lara: *!!!!!!!!!!!!!!*

I assumed this meant we'd passed. She probably was able to access the list before me because she was in California. Either that or she had faster internet speed.

I double-checked. My name was in fact on the list.

A wave of calm washed over me. Then I started thinking about all those mortgage questions and that crazy performance test and started wondering *how the hell did I pass?*

I'd heard that the California Bar is more holistic than other state bar exams (shocker), meaning the administrators will still pass you even if you fail the MBE but your essay scores are high enough. I'm pretty sure this is what happened with me, given how terrible my MBE probably was. And my performance test.

I must have really killed the essays.

Maybe Lara killed the essays, too, or maybe she was just a genius. Because I saw firsthand how little that girl studied. I was incredibly impressed that she passed. I was impressed with both of us. To this day, passing the California Bar Exam is probably my proudest accomplishment. It was really hard, and not everyone did it. But we did it.

I screamed down to my parents, "I passed!"

"Let's pop some champagne," my dad called up the stairs.

"No thanks," I said. "I feel too ill to drink."

I crawled under the covers and slept for fourteen hours.

I woke up feeling relieved but also depressed. I was a lawyer now. I was trapped.

CHAPTER 11

Clerkship

After Trump was elected, a lot of people told me they wished they had gone to law school. The idea that they could have somehow made a difference in American politics if they had gone to law school was a charming—but laughably naive—sentiment.

Everyone entered Berkeley Law wanting to *make a difference*, and I'd been no different. I wanted to give a voice to vulnerable populations fucked over by our appalling criminal justice system. People in my class wanted to save the environment, find housing for the homeless, and provide fair, adequate representation for people with disabilities or those seeking US citizenship. But, for the most part, they all moved on to associate positions in Big Law, shuffling money around between Chinese billionaires. I do not fault them for this. You cannot pay off a $200K debt if your clients are homeless.

Two of my best friends from Berkeley Law, one of whom was heavily addicted to whippits, went into sex work following graduation. When I told a lawyer friend this, she said sex work was "way more dignified than what 90 percent of her law school friends were doing."

She's not wrong.

Berkeley has a progressive reputation, but *Berkeley Law* made you feel like if you didn't leave with a job at a top firm or a clerkship for a federal judge, there was something gravely wrong with you.

Remember: The one thing we all had in common was that failure was our biggest fear. Why do you think we went to law school?

I graduated with a clerkship, but not a federal one.

My professors and the career services people were comically condescending about this.

"I think you're the *only one* with a Superior Court clerkship!" one professor exclaimed, the words "Superior Court" spat out like a slur.

In case you're confused (I was), Superior Court is at the bottom of the food chain, prestige wise. It's where the most important things happen—murder trials, child custody, and so forth—but it's not *elite* and, therefore, I was an embarrassment.

The job began similarly to how my job with Judge Button had. I was panicking about getting a job after graduation because everyone around me was panicking about getting a job. So I called Amber. Amber's dad was good friends with a judge at DC Superior Court who could get me an interview.

I really did not want to move back to DC. I hated it there. I was taking the California Bar Exam so I could stay in California, where I belonged. But I had no other options. I had no interviews in California. No prospects.

I had to pay for my own flight to DC for the interview because the government has no money.

A Big Law firm would have flown me out and put me up in a chichi hotel. Normally, you just clerk for one judge, but this clerkship was for the "senior judges," a group of semiretired judges who rotated on a misdemeanor calendar. It was not a prestigious clerkship.

Three judges interviewed me. One, a friend of Amber's parents, wore cowboy boots, and another was my middle school friend's mom. I was back in the city I grew up in, the place I thought I'd successfully escaped, and I didn't like it.

But I got the job.

———————

I entered my clerkship with a heavy, depressive energy. Luckily, clerkships are only a year long. So I planned to get my clerkship over with quickly, using mostly dissociation and chemical assistance, and head the hell back to California.

I was almost twenty-seven and living with my parents, JD in hand and no life to show for it.

Early in the year of my clerkship, my co-clerk Caitlin told me she hadn't taken the bar yet. You don't need to have passed the bar to get a clerkship. The test results don't come out until most law jobs have already begun. In other law jobs, if you do legal work before you've passed the bar, you just have a licensed attorney sign the filings—as Fernando did for me at the San Francisco Public Defender. We were waiting in line at Panera Bread when I asked Caitlin why she hadn't taken it yet.

"My brother was murdered this summer."

"I'm so sorry," I said. My depression felt very silly in comparison.

My other co-clerk, Evie, didn't pass the bar, so Caitlin and Evie both spent much of the year studying in their cubicles. When I learned Evie hadn't passed the first time, I wasn't shocked. She didn't seem very smart. She would nod vigorously when I spoke, but it was immediately clear she did not understand. Thirty minutes into a conversation she would go, "Ohh, ohhh, ohhhh," and articulate what she thought was a revelation but was simply a basic assumption on which the conversation was premised.

In group conversations, she would repeat—more enthusiastically—what another person had just said. And then she would laugh. She was always laughing. And, like, no one made a joke.

Working with Evie made my depression feel more severe. She was so cheerful.

Evie did nothing all day but drink coffee and make loud attempts at being helpful: "Oh my god, the printer is broken!" For some reason she thought everyone in the office was interested in the trivialities of her life and simply could not keep them to herself: "I'm going downstairs to drop off a file!" or "Jeremy from IT is callllinggggg!" or "My sister has three finals today!"

I would turn my headphones up to the max and she would still stand in my cubicle and yammer on. I couldn't totally hear what she was saying, but I assumed it was weather-related. The weather was Evie's favorite topic because it allowed her to speak without saying anything. Evie was never saying anything, but she was always making noise, whether it was unsolicited updates, chatting, blowing her nose, clearing her throat, or *running* to answer the phone. She reminded me of an animal that hears its owner pick up the leash and dashes toward it.

While our coworkers outwardly admired her "positivity"— "Wow, Evie is always so upbeat!"—I often suspected that they, like me, secretly wanted to put her in a cage.

But I did admire Evie's obvious aversion to doing any actual work. Most of the work was clerical—organizing case files and preparing the calendar. But when it was substantive, I typically did Evie's work for her. I didn't resent this. I only resented the fact that she insisted on talking to me while I did it.

Once, Evie was assigned a bench memo on a semicomplex legal issue. She was stressing about it, so I told her I'd write it for her. Frankly, I was very bored at this job. It's funny, most lawyers complain about being overworked; most of my law jobs were more boring than stressful. Lawyers are insane perfectionists, which is why it's hard for me to believe lawyers when they say they are overworked. Because in law school I saw them working harder than necessary just because their crushing and irrational fear of failure got the best of them.

Anyway, I relished the opportunity to write Evie's memo; it was much more fun than organizing files or answering the phone.

When I finished the memo, I put it on Judge M's desk—the one with the cowboy boots. Later that afternoon, before I left work, I went back to Judge M's office to get a file. I noticed there was a sticky note on the memo.

It said: "Evie agrees!"

I couldn't help but laugh. The audacity! To have me do your work for you, research, write a memo finding a legal conclusion the judge asked *you* to find, and then write a note indicating that you agree. And a smiley face! Did she even read the memo? Did she think the judge would think this meant we worked on it together? Did she think the judge would read it and wonder, "I wonder what Evie thinks. Does she agree?" As if that would be the deciding factor! As if her agreement with a legal issue meant anything at all. She was an idiot!

And while Evie was the bane of my existence, for some reason she was convinced we were best friends. When she got married later that year, she invited me to the rehearsal dinner. I never got invited to rehearsal dinners, but I was invited to Evie's.

One day she came running into my office to show me her bridesmaid dresses. Not just a photo; she was carrying a dress in her arms.

I looked at the lanyard that held the ID I needed to walk around the courthouse and noticed it was the same color as her dress—a very basic, Microsoft Paint blue. I held it up to the dress.

"It's the same color as the lanyard the courthouse gave us," I said. It was a spectacularly rude thing to say. But Evie wasn't even offended.

"You're right!" she squealed.

Being trapped in this office unleashed rage in me. In retrospect, I'm not even sure Evie was that bad. I think she might have just been a target for my angst. I didn't want to be in DC, living with my parents. I didn't want to be wearing a suit and sweating under fluorescent lights, never seeing the sunlight and hardly using my brain. Maybe I just envied Evie. I wished I could be that enthusiastic about answering my work phone. It would make life a lot easier.

I kept busy with lots of side projects—mostly writing self-indulgent personal essays or curating images on Tumblr—to keep myself occupied and distract myself from Evie's noises. Organizing the case files took an hour or two, and I probably had one or two memos a week to write, each of which took a few hours. Then the judges would insist on talking to us for a few more hours a week, for our "edification."

But that still left a *lot* of free time.

So I became very creatively prolific. I wrote almost an entire novel, in the body of a judicial order form. I hired interns to do my research and organize the calendar for me. I created a weekly ritual where we met in the chambers kitchen every Friday afternoon at three to drink beer that was left over from some function. I also got my funniest friend, Beth, to start a blog with me. Beth and I are major haters, so we called our blog "Ubiquitous & Offensive," and posted about popular things we found deeply annoying. Beth's first post was about manatees, and mine was about enthusiasm, but really it was about Evie. I guess she did inspire me. Irritation is a great muse.

On Friday afternoons, well before we were supposed to leave, I'd sneak out the back exit and pretend I was someone else for the weekend—an artist, a writer, an actress. Anyone who didn't have to wear a suit and talk to old white men all day.

Because my time in the office felt like mild torture, I tried my best to make the most of my life outside the office—by spending it nowhere near anything law-related. (Even catching a glimpse of *Law & Order* on television triggered a trauma response.) At a bar one night after work, my high school friend was swiping like mad through a dating app. It was the first time I'd seen a normie like him act casual about internet romance, which I supposed was what Tinder had aspired to do—normalize online dating.

I downloaded the app the next night in my parents' den, the same room where my dad used to smoke cigars. It was all wood paneling and fish-related art—very masculine, an aesthetic I protested by blasting Bravo, the network for women and gays.

Tinder's routine registration process presented a simple question: Are you interested in men, women? Without much thought, I clicked both.

I came across Nat's profile that first night. She was wearing a black silk button-down in front of a white backdrop. Wispy bangs floated across her porcelain skin. She looked smart and angry.

I was smitten.

Before long, we were texting constantly, about everything from Miley Cyrus's *Bangerz* and Bravo's *Shahs of Sunset* to Russian literature and the prison-industrial complex. Nat had been the poet laureate at her college and was getting a master's in cultural studies. She was taking an extra year to finish her dissertation on solitary confinement and had written her application essay about the *Real Housewives* franchise.

Swoon!

Our first date was eight hours long. We met on a Saturday afternoon at a dive bar—I ordered Fireball on the rocks—and ended up at a basement club, where we almost got hate-crimed. We were grinding to Missy Elliott when this man charged at us out of nowhere. "Is that a chick?" he shouted in my face, pointing at Nat. Some of his friends rushed over and held him back.

It was all so exciting! Like I said, I often felt like my privilege meant I deserved to be punished. So in a weird way it felt good to be hate-crimed. It felt like justice.

At the courthouse, one of the administrative assistants—Pam—often made homophobic comments. She often used "gay" as a synonym for "bizarre," which is not something I had heard someone do since I was in middle school. She was also always speculating about peoples' sexuality, like knowing whether they were gay would explain some sort of deficiency she saw. I wasn't sure if she speculated about me, but if not, she should have—given I was talking to my girlfriend 24/7 at work. Sometimes I'd egg Pam into saying very non-PC things, mainly to pass the time. I felt okay about it as a result of my newfound minority status as a practicing lesbian. But I hadn't told anyone at work. I didn't ever talk about my private life at work.

I hung out with the administrative assistants a lot to fill the hours. In addition to Pam, we had Gloria and Ladonna—three middle-aged women with varying degrees of attitude.

Gloria never really wanted to chat. But Pam and Ladonna made up for Gloria's lack of presence.

Pam called herself "the Sheriff" because she was very Law and Order, a Republican in a chambers filled with bleeding-heart liberals. She had no sympathy for the defendants. She wanted them to burn.

The Sheriff also hated being in chambers almost as much as I did. Probably more. She'd been working there for decades and commuted four hours a day to and from her home in rural Maryland. Almost every day, she'd talk about retiring. "I'm almost out of here," she'd say, as she traipsed past my cubicle.

She left the office every afternoon at three, while most people left around six. I really admired her for this, although it seemed to bother everyone else. Pam blamed her commute for her truncated office hours. And in her defense, she always seemed to be the first person in chambers. Although I was rarely there to see it.

Early in my clerkship, I was late to work because I was "tired" (hungover) the day after seeing Kanye West (*Yeezus* tour). From then on, Pam cut out photos of Kanye from whatever rando gossip rag she read on the train and placed them in my cubicle each morning. Eventually, she taped a photo of Kanye onto my nameplate.

Not long after, Judge Robinson—by far the most respectable judge in chambers—showed up in my cubicle with a very serious expression on her face. To be fair, she always had a very serious expression on her face.

"Anna," she said. "Can I talk to you for a minute?"

I was terrified. She terrified me. She was so smart and so austere. She reminded me of Camille from the DPC.

"Of course," I said.

She gestured toward the Kanye photo on my nameplate. "I don't think this is very appropriate."

"Okay," I said, heart racing. "I'll take it down."

She watched me in silence while I threw the photo into the recycling.

"Pam put it here," I said. I wanted Judge Robinson to know it wasn't my idea. "She thought it was funny."

"I don't." Judge Robinson was right.

When I told the other administrator Ladonna what happened, she consoled me. Ladonna was bubbly and positive. Her desk was adorned with children's art and photos of her disabled daughter, who she called "the Diva." The Diva looked like a small child in photos but it turned out she was twenty-one. She couldn't speak, see, or hear. But she *loved* music. In every photo, she wore headphones, no matter what the occasion—a party, her graduation, whatever. I asked Ladonna how the Diva could enjoy music without hearing, and she said the vibrations comforted her.

At the end of the clerkship, I made the Diva a playlist and gave it to Ladonna on a zip drive. Ladonna really inspired me. More than any of the judges did.

One day, Ladonna came into work and announced she had seen Rihanna on TV. "She reminded me of you!" she said.

I was confused but flattered. I am a nerdy white woman and no one has ever compared me to Rihanna before.

"Not the way you look," she said. "But, like, your mannerisms."

At that point, I realized Ladonna had never met a stoner before.

One of the things I hated about living in DC was its annoying attitude toward cannabis. I had been living in California for six years prior to moving back home and was accustomed to walking around with a bowl and a grinder and a plastic bag of squishy green weed in my purse. I was used to smoking it wherever and whenever I wanted. At bars. In public parks. At concerts.

In DC, this didn't fly. Throughout my twenties, I had my purse weed confiscated more times than I can count. Often it came with the threat of arrest, but I was never that scared. Fernando once told me, "Anna, you're lily-white! You would never be arrested!" It stuck with me, and the fact became increasingly glaring and depressing as time went on, as more and more police brutality against people of color came to light. I try to be a good ally, but I'm also human, and I've taken advantage of my skin color to get away with certain things, behavior I consider morally neutral.

Once at a Schoolboy Q concert in DC, I was about to hit the bowl when a security guard came up and took it right out of my hand. Purse weed confiscated, once again.

A few songs later, Schoolboy Q announced, "The security guards are not happy." Then he went into a song that begins: "FUCK THAT!"

I started screaming and jumping up and down while the security guards glared at me.

I felt famous!

But sadly, Schoolboy Q was not at most of my social gatherings in DC that year. Soon after, I was at a party and pulled out my purse weed around a bunch of very drunk people.

"Is that drugs?" someone asked.

I rolled my eyes. "It's not *drugs*," I said, packing my bowl. "It's a plant. It's medicinal."

The man became angry. "No drugs in here," he said. "I get drug-tested for work and I don't want it to pick up any second-hand smoke."

I was shocked and appalled. He was downing whiskey from the bottle. He was wasted to the point he could hardly stand upright. How *dare* he judge me? Secondhand smoke? What a joke!

I missed Berkeley, where you could smoke blunts on campus and where they served weed brownies at school-sponsored events. Where every single party (law school, office, or otherwise) reeked of cannabis. I had been smoking weed at social gatherings for years and really had no idea how to enjoy one without it.

I went home and immediately ordered a portable vaporizer

online. I wasn't going to stop smoking weed at parties, so I knew I had to figure out how to be more discreet.

Every morning I walked into the courthouse with A$AP Ferg's "Murda Something" in my headphones. I went through a metal detector and put my bag through an X-ray machine. I often had weed in my bag. If I was going out after work, I wanted to have it. Luckily, I always got away with it, I assumed because of the combination of my law clerk badge and my bright blonde hair.

"You know the planters outside of the courthouse?" Sheriff Pam asked me once, while she was walking past my cubicle to put case files in the cabinet, a trek she made up to forty times a day.

"Yeah," I said.

"They had to replace them a few years ago because one of the maintenance men realized they were filled with guns and knives and drugs."

"Wow," I said. Probably people had ditched them before going through the X-ray and metal detectors, a desperate move I was privileged enough not to have to engage in.

"Yeah," said Pam. "So many thugs in this place. I can't wait to get out of here." Pam didn't have much awareness of systemic injustice. I didn't fault her for this. She likely had not gone to graduate school.

Lowering my spirits even further, I had to go to misdemeanor court almost every single day.

Misdemeanor court mostly felt like a place to clear the

mentally ill and homeless off the streets. We held a trial for a homeless man who stole a bowl of soup and for a woman who snatched another woman's bracelet. I saw the way the judges favored educated white people who spoke the way lawyers are taught to speak—cold and logical. Whenever a witness revealed a poor grasp of white English, the judge tended to find him or her less credible. I didn't think they were aware they were doing it, but it was painfully obvious as an observer.

In DC, misdemeanor charges are decided by bench trials rather than jury trials, meaning it's all up to the judge. As a clerk, I participated in the deliberations. The other clerks and I would sit in little conference rooms behind the courtroom, or in chambers, and the judges would ask us what we thought. Is there reasonable doubt?

Regardless of what I thought about the evidence, I argued for an acquittal *every single time*. I mean, as I said, our docket mostly comprised petty theft and simple assault, stolen soup and snatched bracelets, things that didn't seem worthy of taxpayer dollars to prosecute.

When a man was charged with taking photos up women's skirts on the subway, I argued it was nonintrusive because he didn't touch the women or make them fear for their lives.

"He was just having fun!" I joked.

No one laughed.

The judge who wore cowboy boots was shocked I took the creep's side.

Six years after the completion of my clerkship, the *Washington Post* published an article and accompanying seven-part audio series accusing the judge with the cowboy boots of sexually assaulting a sixteen-year-old girl when he was thirty-two, just before he became a judge.[1] I wasn't shocked by the allegations; to quote Jenny Holzer, "abuse of power comes as no surprise."[2]

Every day when he got off the bench, the judge would call the clerks into his chambers. He would pour bourbon into one plastic cup and goldfish crackers into another plastic cup and he would drink the bourbon and eat the goldfish and tell us the same stories over and over again. Evie and Caitlin would *ooh* and *ah*, giggle and clap, becoming the Geisha-esque audience he seemed to covet, while I would mostly glare at him, annoyed that I'd have to cancel my happy hour plans. We were making $65,000 a year, nowhere enough for me to stay two hours late to listen to a drunk man babble about his glory years— which I suppose were around the time he was allegedly sexually assaulting this sixteen-year-old girl.

But I was surprised by the angle taken in the *Washington Post* article, which suggested to me that the judge had been too lenient on sex crimes over the years, somehow evincing his alleged guilt. It was a tenuous and surprising suggestion, especially in an era when the liberal media elite seems to agree that the American criminal justice system is overly draconian, particularly on sex crimes.[3] It was also interesting given I'd literally convinced the judge to punish someone less harshly than he wanted to for a sex crime.

I suppose it was unethical of me to argue for an acquittal every single time because I was a lawyer and I wasn't considering the law. But I maintain my actions were not immoral. And as is likely clear at this point, morality is not my primary concern anyway. But I felt like I was doing the right thing. I refused to believe that someone who committed a misdemeanor deserved to be punished. And I refused to believe that locking these people behind bars would do anything to rehabilitate them or protect society.

That year while working as a public defender in San Francisco, Lara said to me, "The fact that it's called the California Department of Corrections disgusts me with its irony." She went on: "I don't believe any thinking person believes that locking someone in a cage in an incredibly dangerous environment makes them a better candidate for society when they reenter."

Amen. For this reason, I became a one-woman jury nullification.

Luckily, I didn't have to deliberate in cases that came before my judges when I had a personal relationship involved. During my clerkship, my best friend and my sister both had DUIs in my courtroom. As if my privilege wasn't loud enough as it was, it went ahead and marched right into my courtroom.

Amber was driving friends home from dinner when another car T-boned her—she was obsessed with the fact that she was T-boned, and kept repeating it over and over when describing the accident—"I was T-boned!"

I suppose she thought it minimized her guilt.

The accident brought the attention of the police, who Breathalyzed her. She told me she had consumed "like, a bottle of wine" that night, which she denied to the officer. The officer had taken her written statement, but he lost the statement, so the case was thrown out in court. (Amber and I are both dying to read the statement, which she wrote while drunk as hell, because it is surely very fucking funny. Unfortunately, due to the officer's incompetence, reading it is not an option.)

I was happy for Amber that her case was thrown out, but a part of me found it depressing. The government was literally always fucking up. Losing shit, lying, racially profiling, tampering with evidence, filing lazy motions, etc. And normally, this misconduct or ineptitude resulted in poor people of color getting locked up. Of course, the one time I hear of a case being dismissed for the government's mistakes, the defendant is a wealthy, well-connected white woman.

Amber and I often fantasized about starting our own law firm. We would call it Anna & Amber LLP, pointedly using our first names in protest of the law's stilted and patriarchal past. We would defend women only who were being punished for nonviolent crimes like theft and DUIs. We would plaster billboards with photos of us arguing in court, and also partying late at night. Our motto would be: *Been there, done that, got out of it.*

My sister got a DUI while visiting DC on a break from college. She was having brunch with her high school friend and drank "four or five 'manmosas'"—orange juice, vodka, beer, and champagne. On the way home, she was pulled over and Breathalyzed. She blew a .23. According to my Google search, a blood alcohol level of this magnitude suggests having consumed around ten drinks in a two-and-a-half-hour period.[4]

My sister's case was also dismissed, for prosecutorial laziness. While I was happy for my sister, it felt unfair for the same reason Amber's case did. I had been watching the government with zero hesitation zealously pursue cases against poor people of color all year. And, again, when the defendant was a wealthy white woman, suddenly they didn't have time.

If you haven't witnessed a trial, I'd highly recommend it. The clerks were encouraged to watch trials in other courtrooms for our edification, so I watched as many as my schedule allowed.

At DC Superior Court I became engrossed in a trial happening in another courtroom.

The details of the case—an eccentric German con artist accused of murdering his socialite wife—sounded familiar when another clerk mentioned it at one of our mandatory meetings. I later realized I'd read a longform article on the murder a few years prior. It often takes several years for a murder case to actually get to trial.

Albrecht Muth met his victim, Viola Drath, forty-four years his senior, when he was a teenage intern for a Republican senator and she was an established journalist. Albrecht told her he was a fan of her column and asked her to dinner. Viola was intrigued by him—both of their families had fled East Germany. After Viola's husband died, Albrecht started coming to her house every day and eventually proposed.

When they married in 1990, Viola was seventy and Albrecht was twenty-six.

After they married, Albrecht made up a story about an elderly German count who had fallen from an elephant in India and appointed him, Albrecht, as his successor. After that, he insisted on going by Count Albrecht. (Very Luann de Lesseps.) Then in 2003, after the Iraq War, Albrecht suddenly adopted the rank and began wearing the uniform of a brigadier general in the Iraqi Army.

Put simply: Albrecht was nutty.

Albrecht's theatrics continued into his murder trial. As soon as he was arrested, he started going on hunger strikes that landed him in the hospital. He said he was fasting because of orders he had received from Archangel Gabriel. Before trial, his doctor said that he was too physically weak to appear in the courtroom.

The Constitution guarantees the accused the right to be present at his or her trial, but as with everything in the law, there are exceptions. Fed up with all the delays, the trial judge found that Albrecht "knowingly and voluntarily and intelligently" waived his right to be present at trial. He would be able to watch the proceedings live from his hospital bed via Skype.

There was some talk in the courtroom that Albrecht might testify over Skype, but sadly, for my rubbernecking ass, that did not happen.

During trial, a number of witnesses from Viola's family and social circle testified that Albrecht was physically and emotionally abusive. Witnesses testified to seeing bruises on Viola's neck and seeing Albrecht chastise Viola and even lay his hands on her. Witnesses also suggested that Albrecht's motives were financial, which Albrecht didn't totally deny.

"We had a marriage of convenience," Albrecht told the police just after Viola's death. "We got along contentiously."

Months before Viola's murder, Viola's daughters had received a bunch of frantic emails from Albrecht with a list of things he wanted when Viola died. The daughters were alarmed because their mother was perfectly healthy. And then, on the day of Viola's death, Albrecht purportedly gave Viola's daughter a document asking for $150,000 to be put in his name.

Albrecht's Google searches before the murder were shown to include the words "prenuptials," "extradition from Mexico," and "flights."

Oh, and he'd been drinking heavily with a man he met on Craigslist the very night of his wife's death.

In other words, evidence that Albrecht killed Viola, or at least had a hand in her death, was *overwhelming*.

Without Viola's money, Albrecht qualified for the public defender to defend him. DC Public Defender Service (PDS), where I had interned, was among the best public defender offices in the country. So good, in fact, that I almost started to believe Viola's death was an accident during the defense closing. (The defense didn't put on any witnesses—which suggests to most people that the defendant is guilty—so the closing was all we got.)

Like most PDS closings, this one began with an alliterative set of three words. Something along the lines of "dubious, doubtful, disbelief." This is a trick they taught us during our trial practice class when I interned there. PDS's style is famously theatrical and ruthless.

The defense stressed that there were no eyewitnesses, and no DNA or forensic evidence. Also, Viola was old. She was found dead in her bathroom and could have slipped. It is the government's burden to prove guilt beyond a reasonable doubt, and the defense argued that did not occur here, when Viola's death could have just as likely been an accident.

The jury disagreed and after deliberating for less than one day found Albrecht guilty.

But in my memory the theatrics took precedence over any legal or factual issues. It was like watching a movie. That is the way criminal trials work. Theatrics distract and obscure. In law school, they teach you trials are about finding facts. The judges said that, too. But I didn't buy it. Trials are about emotional manipulation. Trial is performance. I started to see this with Judge Button, but the notion was cemented during my clerkship.

I'd also always known that the criminal justice system operated differently when the defendant had money, but during my clerkship, I saw this firsthand over and over again, starting with my best friend's and sister's DUI dismissals. Most noteworthy was when Chris Brown's assault case appeared on our docket. I was never a Chris Brown fan, but I knew he had dated Rihanna, and even though their relationship was tumultuous, I clung to the possibility that Rihanna might unexpectedly show up at the courthouse. This far-fetched fantasy got me through my mundane, fluorescent-lit days. My desire to see Rihanna trumped my desire for her to avoid her domestic abuser. I felt guilty about it, but I didn't stop wanting her to show.

The "incident" occurred during Howard University's homecoming. According to the testimony, Chris was leaving his hotel when some girls came up and asked to take a photo with him. He agreed. During the photo taking, one girl's male friend tried to jump in, at which point Chris became aggressive.

"I'm not down with that gay shit," he said. And then he punched the man in the face.

Chris's bodyguard was his codefendant.

With Chris's trial, everything was different. Suddenly, the motions were really good—well organized, well written, thorough—clearly the work of fancy private attorneys who were being adequately compensated, probably overcompensated, for their time. Normally, I didn't even read the motions when writing an order because they were so lazy and unhelpful, making arguments like "the search was illegal because it did not follow legal protocol." Government attorneys are overworked and underpaid. I didn't blame them for writing sloppy motions, but I knew I could research the law faster and more effectively myself. (Or my interns could.)

At the end of one day of reading pleadings, I peeked into the cowboy-boot judge's chambers.

"You know Chris Brown has a tattoo of a battered Rihanna on his neck," I said without really thinking. I didn't know at the time that it was completely unethical of me to say this—judges aren't supposed to do any independent research or consume any outside information on the parties to a case that could color their decision making. But I guess I just wanted the judge to know Chris Brown was a scumbag. He was the only defendant who entered our courtroom who I wanted to be found guilty, who I wanted to be punished. I finally understood where Pam was coming from with all her defendant-directed rage.

"I'm going to pretend I didn't hear that," the judge said.

Although the judges typically heard up to forty matters per day, when Chris had a hearing, the calendar was completely cleared. A PR person stepped in to manage the courtroom and reserve seats for journalists and celebrities.

Again, I was wrapped up in the theater of the proceedings. The PR woman would save a row of seats for my interns and me in the gallery so we could watch. I kept hoping Rihanna would come.

One day during a pretrial hearing, I returned from lunch to see Ladonna and Evie chatting. Ladonna said, "Anna, you missed Rihanna!"

"Yeah," said Evie. "You just missed her!"

I immediately started crying.

"Oh my god," Ladonna said. "We're kidding. We had no idea you would take it so seriously." Evie tried to hug me and I pushed her off. I was *so* depressed.

Eventually, Chris took a plea. His bodyguard was tried and found guilty. We speculated that Chris paid off his bodyguard to take the fall for him, because over the course of the pretrial hearings, the testimonies changed to reflect that the bodyguard actually threw the punch.

It was a perfect example of how the criminal justice system works. The poor and desperate take the fall while the rich go free, unscathed.

I wanted out.

CHAPTER 12

Escape Plan

Judge Walker, my favorite judge, typically wore a sweatsuit and—I kid you not—*slippers* under her judicial robes. She worked in family court and *loved* the drama. Often, she'd return to chambers howling.

"Ooohhhh, you clerks missed a *scene* down in family court today."

I like to think she picked me as her confidant because I'm special, but really it was because my cubicle was the closest to her office.

One morning she rolled in at ten (court starts at nine) and called my name down the small hallway to my cubicle as she stood outside her office door. "Anna," she said. "I feel like Cameron Diaz in *Bad Teacher* right now." Then she cackled.

"What do you mean?" I asked. "I haven't seen it."

She lowered her voice to a whisper. "I'm hungover," she said, then cackled again.

When I found out I had passed the bar, I needed a judge to

swear me in. It could be any judge, so I asked Judge Walker. She was thrilled. She read a script while I raised my right hand and repeated after her. Kind of like I was getting married.

Afterward, she beamed. "I wish we had some wine!"

Judge Walker *loved* wine. She talked about it all the time, almost as much as she talked about the rapper Remy Ma, most famous for her work with Fat Joe's Terror Squad and her public feuds with Foxy Brown and Nicki Minaj.

"Anna, I heard you like rap music," she said one day. "My daughter is friends with Remy Ma."

"Oh cool," I said. "Isn't she in prison?" (This was 2014.)

"Yeah," said Judge Walker. "It's a real shame."

"What did she do, again?" I asked.

Judge Walker lowered her voice to a whisper. "Shot someone." She paused. "But it's complicated."

A few months later, Judge Walker skipped into chambers. "Remy Ma is getting out todayyyyy," she sang.

"Oh," I said, "great." I wasn't sure what to say... *Congratulations?*

Another day, Judge Walker called me into her office and then asked me to shut the door.

"Anna, I need you to help me with something," she said. "You can't tell any of the other judges that I'm asking you to do this."

"You got it," I agreed. I was excited.

"I want to apply for another job," she said. "I'm over being a judge."

"I get that," I said.

"I saw a job posting from University of Maryland. They're hiring a criminology professor. I want to apply, but I haven't written a cover letter in forty years. Also, I need an updated résumé."

"I can help you," I said.

"Great," she said.

She gave me some materials and I hopped on preparing her application. I weirdly love writing cover letters; they're basically just personal essays. But Judge Walker didn't give me much to work with, so I was struggling.

The next day, I returned to her office.

"So, I have a question for the cover letter," I said.

"Shoot."

"Why do you want to be a criminology professor?"

She scrunched her nose. "Wait," she said. "What *is* criminology again?"

I tried not to laugh. "It's like studying crime in a scientific way. I think it's a lot of statistics."

"Science? Math?" she said. "Ew! Never mind. I don't want to do that." I sympathized. After witnessing the daily chaos of superior court, who could revert to the banalities of systematized knowledge?

I didn't want to end up like Judge Walker, to wake up one day in my mid-sixties and make my law clerk write my escape letter, only to realize I didn't have any marketable skills.

Writing was my escape that year. It was the only place I felt confident and excited and in control. I'd started to feel that the legal system was broken beyond repair, and that continued to depress me. The law seemed to be primarily concerned with thoughtlessly reinforcing existing power structures, administered by lawyers who were thoughtlessly chasing gold stars. I felt like I could make a bigger difference writing entertaining things that could make people laugh or think differently or distract them through their mundane days.

I wanted to be able to write more and to do it undisturbed, on my own time. In a T-shirt or maybe just a bra. Without constant interruptions and expectations. That was probably an unrealistic goal, but I had plenty of time on my hands to dream. I'd passed the California Bar Exam at twenty-six and wanted a new challenge.

But I needed a plan.

———

When my clerkship ended, I was thrilled. Not having a job really suited me. I was still living with my parents, so I didn't need to worry about paying rent. I was free to fuck around for a bit.

I started a routine I still keep today, five years later: Wake up. Make coffee. Write for two or three hours. Exercise. Eat lunch and watch reality TV or YouTube. Sometimes nap. Make more coffee. Write for two or three more hours. Open a beer. Write for thirty minutes. Vape. Open another beer. Write for another hour. Then either go out or return to reality TV.

A dream!

It was my favorite time of year in DC—mid-August, when the nights were hot and the city emptied out as residents flocked to their summer houses. I could walk to bars in a dress, vape along the way, arrive with a dewy face. Without work, I could go outside during the day, so I was tan and high off all the vitamin D.

My best friends from law school were mostly working their asses off at law firms. One day while I was out and about and feeling just terrific, Spencer texted me: Elizabeth Wurtzel just screamed at me in the elevator.

Who? I wrote back. I'm embarrassed to write that I didn't know who she was.

She wrote Prozac Nation, he texted back. I'd heard of that book, but I was more familiar with the movie starring Christina Ricci.

Why is she at your office? I asked.

She works here, he wrote. Then he sent me an article for *The Cut* she'd written the previous year in which she explained how she was a "free spirit" and went to law school (Yale) on a "lark," then ended up working at Boies Schiller, with Spencer. I was intrigued. I'd always been fascinated with Yale, and there was no school harder to get into than Yale Law. And I loved her writing, which was cocky and brazen. She wrote that her major claim to adulthood was that she no longer did bumps of cocaine before running. My favorite portion was about being a lawyer:

> Most people who think they are practicing law are actually making binders, and my guess is that most people who think they are doing whatever important thing they are doing are making binders. The binders from law firms go to a locker in a warehouse in a parking lot in an office park off an exit of a turnpike off a highway off an interstate in New Jersey, never to be looked at again. No one ever read them in the first place. But some client was billed for the hourly work.[1]

That resonated. At my clerkship, I didn't make binders, but I did make case files, which were just smaller binders. I recalled Evie introducing me at her housewarming party as her "colleague," which felt bizarrely formal considering we were drinking moonshine at the time. She always seemed to think that what she was doing was very important. Everyone in DC did.

Before I knew it, it was September. For my birthday, I went to California to look for jobs. I *needed* to get back to California. I was twenty-eight and felt like a failson for living with my parents.

That fall, Emily and Spencer visited me in DC from New York. They stayed with me at my parents' house, or as my sister and I call it when we have guests—Camp Dorn.

Watching Spencer calculate his billable hours one morning at the breakfast table, my mom practically salivated. She assumed the same eager expression she took on when my friend Amber would talk to her about trying to make partner. It seemed Mom was slipping into the fantasy that these ambitious big-firm lawyers were her offspring instead of me.

"So amazing of you to work so hard on a Saturday morning," my mom said with a mixture of excitement and dissatisfaction, apparently exhilarated by the fantasy and upset that it was only a fantasy, wondering where she had gone wrong as a mother.

Being the disappointment I was, I trudged upstairs to sleep off my hangover.

Later that afternoon, over drinks, Spencer said, "Your mom is so funny."

"Really?" I asked. My mom is a lot of things—reserved, elegant, discerning—but *funny* isn't a word that comes to mind. My sister and I often laugh *at* her, but this is more a defense mechanism than anything else. Laugh or be wounded.

"She came over to me all frantic while I was working this morning," he said. "And she started interrogating me about you, and about how you've been talking about wanting to be a writer. She's really worried. She was like," he paused, making his eyes all big, slightly altering his voice to sound more feminine, "'Is Anna...okay?'"

I laughed really hard. His impression of my mom was dead-on. I could see her saying it.

But it really wasn't that funny.

Since I was a kid, my mom has always been serving hard "is Anna okay?" energy in my direction.

I have vivid memories of being on the soccer field. Other parents would cheer on their kids from the sidelines. My mom would stand nervously and whisper to me as I ran past, "Anna, are you okay?" I guess she thought I wasn't playing very well.

When I told my mom I wanted to be a writer, she compared me to a basket weaver.

And when I told her about this book deal, she said I'd made a "deal with the devil."

She's incapable of seeing me as anything but a failure, which I suppose is where I get my abysmal self-worth.

I've since let go of my sadness at being such a disappointment to my mom. I know her anxiety comes from a place of love, and she is just trying her best to give me a good life. My mom wanted me to be a career woman because she grew up in a time and place when having a career wasn't presented as an option to her. She wanted desperately for me to be what she couldn't be. But she never considered what I wanted to be. And when I didn't want what she wanted, she took it as a personal attack.

But it was hard being in a house with that energy 24/7 when I already hated myself. I needed to get back to California, which was—conveniently—three thousand miles from my mom's disapproval.

I got an interview with a San Francisco law firm called Rosen Bien Galvan & Grunfeld, a "good" law firm known for suing prisons. Actually, Rhonda—my kooky Advanced Legal Writing teacher—had worked there in the 1990s. I was shocked they wanted to interview me, and definitely did not expect to get the job. This was a very HLS job. And I was a midtier Berkeley grad.

As anticipated, they didn't seem very interested in me during the interview. In a conversation with one of the partners (honestly, I can't tell you which, but I can promise he was an older Jewish man), I got the sneaking suspicion that he deeply hated me.

"What do you do for fun?" he asked.

"I write," I said.

"What do you write?" he asked.

"Personal essay and memoir-type stuff," I said. Very eloquent.

"Memoir?" he basically spit. "You aren't old enough to write a memoir. You've hardly lived!" He looked like he might lunge at me.

"I guess you're right," I said, then looked at my lap to avoid his angry glare.

(*Well, look at me now, Mr. Rosen, Bien, Galvan, or Grunfeld!*)

After the interview, I took the BART to Berkeley and had drinks with my old supervisor from the Death Penalty Clinic, Amit (Mr. Nine on the Enneagram). We met at a biergarten at two that afternoon, a plan that suited me well. I told him that

I had applied to an MFA program (just one, because it was the only one I found in California that didn't require GREs), but that I needed to get a job in the meantime. And that I probably wasn't going to get the one I'd just interviewed for. Three beers in, he told me that his wife had just received funding to hire a research fellow to study juvenile life without parole (JLWOP). I was interested.

Then, poof, his wife came to meet up with us. Like the whole thing had been planned. His wife was this modelesque Australian woman who cared deeply about criminal justice. They'd met working on death penalty cases in New Orleans. A match made in neoliberal heaven.

I had to pretend to be more sober than I was while she told me about the fellowship. She said that the United States is the only developed country that sentences juveniles to life in prison. Then she told me that the fellow would work remotely, as if it was a bad thing, and that I would have a lawyer supervisor named Paul. The fellowship would last for one year.

I was hooked. My delusional brain made a plan right then and there in the middle of my buzz: By the time the fellowship year was over, my writing career would have taken off. I'd never have to be a lawyer again! This job was perfect! It would also get me back to California and give me the time I needed to find an agent and sell a book. I needed this job. I *needed* this job. I told her I was interested about twenty times and then excused myself to go to a party.

I moved to Oakland in mid-November. I was hired for the remote JLWOP fellowship. I also was accepted into the MFA program. I decided to defer my MFA acceptance for a year so I could complete the fellowship first and therefore dedicate more time to it. Besides, I would have sold a book by then, hopefully, before the master's program started. So I'd enter the program, like, famous.

Delusions Rule Everything Around Me. (DREAM!)

I found an amazing studio apartment in a charming Tudor building near Lake Merritt. The previous tenant had died in the apartment, which was a little ominous, but the views made up for it. You could say they were *to die for*. (Sorry that was tasteless.) It was on the seventh floor and looked over downtown Oakland. From the fire escape, I could even see the lake.

Shortly after I moved in, I met my legal supervisor Paul for lunch in San Francisco. He was a tall, thin hipster. He looked like most public interest lawyers do. He wore jeans and a button-down, had dark circles under his eyes, and carried a backpack instead of a briefcase. He told me about his appellate practice and about the fellowship. I tried to appear interested. After lunch, I met some friends and got drunk.

The fellowship, which would start that Monday, involved writing a report on JLWOP laws and policies in all fifty states. I would include a small section on each state, summarizing the state of the law and major JLWOP cases there. It was actually an enjoyable mix of tedium and thinking. Much like most legal assignments.

I'd work on the report during the day, and when five o'clock hit, I'd open a beer and work on my personal writing as the sky turned Technicolor. Then I'd go out, normally on a date.

I went on a lot of dates that year. I didn't have many friends. Spencer and Emily were in New York. Lara had just experienced a traumatic brain injury—she fell while running down the marble courthouse stairs on no sleep during a trial—so she couldn't do much. When she was unable to use her brain, the public defender office had her just sit at the defense table during rape trials, mostly because juries are less likely to convict an alleged rapist when they see a female attorney defending him. Otherwise, she would sleep. She wasn't even allowed to read, which, for a genius like Lara, was torture.

So Tinder became my social life.

It was mostly pretty sad. I was excited about a few dates, like the girl with whom I communicated exclusively in Drake lyrics—*I need to know, where do you wanna go? Cause if you're down, I'll take it slow*—before we met up IRL.

But the date was a big disappointment. We had the chemistry of, like, a cat and a fish. She started the date by telling me about a rash she had all over her body, and for some reason I stayed for five beers. In my twenties, I was mostly going on dates with alcohol.

Paul also had me work on one of his death penalty cases from Arizona. Honestly, I don't remember the facts of the case at all, but I do remember that the state of Arizona paid my checks.

Here are some things the state of Arizona paid me to do: text my friends, drink kombucha while watching palm trees sway outside my window, develop my "Twitter voice," look at paparazzi photos of Mary-Kate Olsen, write blog articles for a men's fashion website, and make Spotify playlists with corny titles like "trap queen" and "oaklandia."

I must have done some legal work during that time, but I have no specific memory of it.

This is precisely why I oppose the death penalty.

We were at the postconviction phase, or habeas, which mostly involved digging up facts from the defendant's past that might not have arisen at trial.

Paul flew me to Phoenix to interview witnesses about the defendant's childhood. The goal was to find something—*anything*—to put the defendant in a positive light and mitigate his crime before a court. I was paired with a man named Tim, a current Berkeley Law student who would later replace me when my fellowship ended. Tim was an older law student, around forty. He'd previously lived in New York and made documentaries. He had a master's in journalism and had worked with Al Maysles, who made my favorite movie, *Grey Gardens*. I thought Tim was very cool and felt blessed to be paired with him. He chain-smoked Parliament Lights, the brand I smoked when I was drunk and feeling bad.

We were tasked with interviewing the leader of the gang our defendant was involved in, a man named Sancho. To qualify for the death penalty, a crime has to have certain "aggravating factors." In this case, one of these aggravating factors was that the crime was gang-related. On habeas, we wanted to argue that the alleged "gang" was more of a "club." You know, to make it seem like it wasn't really on the level of a sophisticated criminal enterprise as imagined by the death penalty statute.

"Last time I went to see Sancho," Tim said on the drive, "he was really methed out."

"How did you know?" I asked. I'd never seen someone on meth.

"It was obvious based on his appearance," Tim said without skipping a beat. "He was fidgety, had dilated pupils, rapid eye movement, sudden outbursts."

"Damn, someone did his research," I said. I was charmed by his lawyerly explanation of meth abuse. Some girls like poetry, but I prefer a precise description of a narcotic's effect.

"I used to be addicted to meth," he said.

"Oh." I felt stupid.

"I was gay in New York in the nineties," he said, "so..."

Tim was so cool.

"He was washing his car and seemed pretty amped up," he said. "When we asked to talk to him, he just took the hose and pointed it at his face, and started spraying himself like crazy."

I laughed at the image.

But I was also kind of afraid.

Sancho wasn't home when we arrived at his bleak Phoenix suburban home, which was surrounded by brightly colored lawn ornaments. I was mostly relieved and ready to go, but Tim wanted to stay a bit longer and wait. Eventually, Sancho came charging down the street. Even from a few blocks away he looked pissed. He was carrying a Big Gulp in one hand and what looked like a metal pipe in the other.

"What do you want?" he asked when he got closer. Then he started running at us. One look at the metal pipe and I ran toward the car. I felt like a baby, but, to be fair, *he was running at us with a metal pipe.* Tim stayed a bit longer but eventually followed my lead.

"He doesn't seem to be in the mood to chat," he said serenely when he met me at the car. I was amazed by how calm Tim was.

Ultimately, we didn't get any useful information about the defendant on that trip from any of our leads, but I returned to Oakland with a new friend and a lot of stories.

Totally worth the Arizona tax dollars.

Back in the Bay, Paul told me I wasn't making progress quickly enough on the JLWOP report and had to speed it up. I had previously been doing one state a week, and he told me I needed to complete at least three states a week. I was up for the challenge.

But that summer, Paul's wife had a baby and he took paternity leave. This meant I had three months practically unsupervised. The report was basically done; I just had to make a spreadsheet organizing the data. So I worked on my novel about a postconviction capital case, which obviously involved a lesbian love triangle. I sent it out to agents, a few of whom asked to read it, but none of whom wanted to represent me.

My query letter announced I was "seeking representation for my debut forty-seven-thousand-word novel entitled LEN'S FLARE, a hip, nihilistic thriller, equal parts Gillian Flynn and Brett Easton Ellis." So delusional. Also, forty-seven thousand words is more of a novella than a novel. I had no idea what I was doing.

(By the way, the query letter went like this: "Blanca Campbell is scheduled to be executed by the state of Arizona in twenty-seven days." I wonder where I got that idea. "It follows Ms. Campbell's legal team in the days leading up to the execution. With a critical eye and detached perspective," I wrote, "Quinn watches as the team of lawyers and psychologists scramble to find that shining piece of trauma, anything to convince the court that Blanca Campbell's life should be spared. The novel explores exploitation and voyeurism, documenting professionals high on the notion that they're saving lives while advancing their careers, enjoying a twisted satisfaction from glimpses into a more dangerous existence." Hmmm, how inventive!)

When Paul returned from paternity leave, we had to actually finish the report. Paul wanted to get it published, and we needed data for that, but I kept zoning out and losing my place while working on the spreadsheet. So he hired a Cornell PhD student in statistics to help us.

By the end of the fellowship, we finished the report, which we called *No Hope*. So fun.

We found that although only nine states had fully abolished JLWOP, in practice, few other states actually imposed JLWOP. The fact that a lot of states didn't use it mattered to the Supreme Court, which we hoped would see this report, because we hoped the report would be cited in an amicus brief, a brief that is filed by nonlitigants with a strong interest in the subject matter. If a given punishment violates the "national consensus"—in other words, if the punishment is unpopular—the Supreme Court is more likely to find it violates the Eighth Amendment. We found that just nine states accounted for 82 percent of all JLWOP sentences, which was good for building national consensus against it. We also found that Black juveniles arrested for homicide were twice as likely to be sentenced to JLWOP than their white counterparts, which was bad, but good for the argument that this sentence should be abolished—because it was unfairly imposed. We found more things, too, but they are dry and I will not bore you.

We wrote a law review article based on the report and, near the end of my fellowship, it was accepted for publication. And I'd completed another yearlong law job. Jobless again, and happy about it.

Except for the fact that I hadn't sold a book yet.

CHAPTER 13

Unhinged and Jobless

My writing career, to my dismay, was not a career at all. The only writing I was being paid to do was about Illinois DUI law. Under the pen name Margot Fontaine, I wrote personal essays about my Tinder social life for a now-defunct blog no one read. I'd queried, maybe, a thousand agents. I pitched *The Cut* and *Buzzfeed* and *Vice* every week.

Nada.

I had a few friends from college in LA and visited all the time. I fantasized about moving there full-time. LA was unhinged and haunting in a way that appealed to me. Everyone seemed to be on the verge of a mental breakdown. I liked that. The Bay was tepid by comparison, its technocrat inhabitants becoming more intolerable by the day. Yes, the air was cleaner and the geographic beauty was unparalleled, but dusty, apocalyptic LA felt more like home.

Also, my MFA program was there. It was a low-residency program, meaning I had to be physically on campus only for five 10-day-long residencies. Everything else was online, so I could live anywhere. But it would be nice not to have to travel for the residencies.

(Although, when I moved to LA, I realized that driving from Echo Park to Culver City *is travel*.)

A few months before my job ended, I posted an event on my Google Calendar that said: MOVE TO LA UNLESS YOU HAVE AN AMAZING REASON NOT TO!!!!!!!!!!!!! Thirteen exclamation points. The event was scheduled for January 4, 2016, from seven to nine a.m.

And I kept the appointment. On that morning, I packed up my car and drove to LA. I moved in with my college friend Rex, who was about to start a job in the art department on *Transparent* and who had found us a cute two-bedroom in Echo Park. The first night I moved in, we binged-watched *Transparent*. Rex had never seen it, but I was a huge Jill Soloway fan and hoped Rex's new job would enable me to seduce Jill. This never happened, even after I showed up basically naked to the *Transparent* wrap party.

I was thrilled to be living in Los Angeles, where every turn held the promise of meeting someone hot and famous who could bring me up to their ranks. I was thrilled with my Tinder prospects—glamorous, creative women who felt worlds away from the backpacking tech workers of the Bay Area. The first person I matched with—I kid you not—invited me to the Golden Globes.

For our first date.

Clare was a power bitch with a brown bob, expensive-looking suits, and a thin frame. I don't typically like thin women, but she was an agent for TV writers and some fiction writers and had represented a number of famous ones.

I was beyond desperate for an agent, and the only way I knew how to get anything in the professional world was to charm someone over drinks, and I wasn't above fucking my way up to the top.

I said no to the Golden Globes. It felt a little high-stakes for a first date.

"What if I'm some kind of psycho?" I wrote to her. "I could jeopardize your whole career."

"I know you aren't," she said. "I can tell we'll get along."

Clare had a kind of creepy, algorithmic vibe that intrigued me. Perhaps it was a necessity to function in Hollywood. She was like one of those law school women who were hyper-invested in playing the game. A lot of agents are former lawyers.

We met for drinks at Black Cat, a run-of-the-mill Silver Lake bar. After drinks, she took me to her friend's house to pregame a lesbian party in West Hollywood. I wondered whether she invited a Tinder date to every event she attended.

Her friends were cool and normal, and confirmed that my date was not. They told me Clare had a mannequin collection. She was, aptly, a serial dater—I would expect anyone with a mannequin collection to be a serial something. She didn't have many friends, and I assumed she liked me because I can be as vacant as a doll.

I don't remember much about the party except there was a lot of glitter and butterflies and asymmetrical haircuts and neon paint. At the end of the night, I slipped on the paint and took a big tumble. Clare was nice about it and helped me up.

I ended the night feeling lukewarm about Clare, but I still wanted to charm her. I wanted an agent. (Shit, I suppose I was playing the game, too.) And I was delusional enough to think that a woman who represented multiple Emmy winners would represent me—a true nobody. But who gets anywhere without a little delusion? That week, Clare took me to an exclusive comedy show for industry people and then drove me home in her Mercedes.

For the next date, Clare invited me to Palm Springs. I had a party to attend that weekend, and this was back when I enjoyed attending parties, so I declined Clare's invitation. She seemed pissed. "Come on," she said. "It will be so romantic." I was flattered but a little confused. We had gone on two dates—why was she talking about romance? On Saturday night when I was drinking with my friends, she texted, come to Palm Springs. I'll call you an Uber. This was hot but a little insane. She hardly knew me. I said I couldn't make it, but I was excited to see her when she got back.

Then she ghosted me.

Even though I didn't feel much chemistry with Clare, I was sad to be ghosted. I was twenty-nine and wanted everyone I dated to fall in love with me, or else it would reveal something terrible about me. It was the same way I felt about passing the bar exam. I require excessive amounts of external validation, an issue I've been working on in therapy since I was eleven.

Aside from being ghosted, I was thrilled to be living in the City of Angels.

I started writing for Justia—basically, Wikipedia for law—and it kept me busy and helped me pay bills. That said, my editor often told me that my posts were messy and difficult to edit. It wasn't the first time I'd heard this from an editor, and it wouldn't be the last. I'd rush through assignments, mostly so I could get to my creative writing, which was what I preserved all my energy for. For this reason, I wasn't the best employee. My creative writing always came first. It's all I thought about. Everything else was just a paycheck.

(When I recently reached out to Justia for more freelance work, they declined.)

Shortly after I moved to LA, I received a press release from my former office announcing that in the recent opinion *Montgomery v. Louisiana*, the U.S. Supreme Court had decided protections against mandatory JLWOP applied retroactively. For context, the Supreme Court had invalidated mandatory JLWOP in *Miller v. Alabama*. Put simply, LWOP is mandatory under some sentencing schemes for certain types of crimes, like killing a cop. And when a juvenile was charged as an adult for such a crime, the defendant could get LWOP and the court would have no say over it. But in *Miller*, the Court decided that mandatory JLWOP violated the Eighth Amendment prohibition on cruel and unusual punishment because it precluded the judge from considering the juvenile's maturity level and other relevant factors.

And in *Montgomery*, the Court held that Miller applied to sentences made final before Miller was decided in 2012. Therefore, any juvenile in the United States who was serving a mandatory LWOP sentence—no matter when it was ordered—was entitled to a rehearing. In many ways, this was a win.

But my boss was disappointed the Court didn't take the opportunity to strike down JLWOP in its entirety.

I didn't feel any type of way about it. As with most Supreme Court decisions, *Montgomery* felt bogus, like a charade. A bunch of noise. Symbolic at best. The criminal justice system would remain cruel and unusual. It would remain racist, with or without JLWOP—mandatory or discretionary.

Not to mention the world of law felt far away from me. I was busy writing another novel, loosely inspired by the Kardashians.

———

My MFA program was very chill. I got to do what I did normally—write self-indulgent things and have obnoxious opinions about books—for master's credit. A lot of people complained about the workload, which I found hilarious—especially after law school. If you find it challenging to produce twenty pages of fiction, read two books, and write two short papers on them a month, I thought, you probably shouldn't be getting an MFA. It's not like it's a practical degree. It's not like there's any big prize on the other side.

For my first residency, I had a very chic and slender professor named Francesca Lia Block. She's famous for *Weetzie Bat*, a cult YA series set in dreamy punk Los Angeles. I never read it, but I never told anyone that.

I didn't read much as a child. When I was growing up, books didn't interest me. They always seemed to star boy-crazy, frumpy girls with poor emotional regulation. They took place in New England or Old England or the past. Books were earnest and lacked humor and had nothing to do with me. I much preferred *Saved by the Bell*.

(In college I discovered Bret Easton Ellis and Joan Didion. Their sentences were exciting, but not gushy. Their characters didn't cry; they numbed out with drugs. They wrote about beautiful people and dark subject matter. I wanted to do what they did.)

I thought Francesca was just the coolest and smartest woman alive. (Whether I had a sex dream about her is neither here nor there.) And she seemed to like my Kardashian book, which felt amazing. When she compared my main character to Maria Wyeth, the protagonist of Joan Didion's *Play It as It Lays*, I cried—which, *trust*, is not something I do regularly.

After class I'd have my college friend Jake over to my new apartment in Echo Park and we'd drink beers while I gushed about Francesca. We'd also talk about my weird LA dates, like about that creepy agent who offered to Uber me to Palm Springs.

"I bet she was going to kill you," he said.

I laughed. "I don't think she's *that* kind of crazy."

"You don't know that," he said. He raised his thick brows. "This would be a good screenplay."

Jake was an aspiring screenplay writer, and I'd always wanted to write something with him.

"Oh my god, you're right," I said. "Let's write it."

And so we started outlining our erotic lesbian thriller.

I finally felt like I was in the right place.

Jake legitimately thought someone was going to kill me and he didn't want to do anything about it except turn it into a contemporary *Basic Instinct*. Ironically, twisting my reality into something entertaining for future mass consumption felt like the most authentic thing I could do.

And I was finally doing it. I noticed that my depression was lifting. I was seeing the light at the end of the tunnel. My escape plan was hatching.

CHAPTER 14

Bedroom Lawyer

I loved all my creative writing projects, but I had to make money.

I applied to be on all of California's criminal appellate panels. California has six appellate districts, and each hires a panel of attorneys to take appeals on the state's dime. Thanks to the Constitution, everyone convicted of a crime is entitled to one appeal, and if they can't afford an attorney, the state is required to provide one.

I was accepted to three panels.

A certain number of my first cases would be assisted by a supervising attorney until I would go out on my own.

Because I was inexperienced, most of my cases were misdemeanors or nonviolent felonies, meaning my clients weren't locked up by the time they were assigned to me—they had mostly finished serving their time. Sometimes they didn't even serve time, just community service. Most of them seemed to have no interest whatsoever in their appeal—they should have called it their unappeal.

I did the work from my bedroom, making it all the more removed. The panel office would send me the record file and a memo from my supervisor outlining the issues. The appeals courts couldn't find a way to get me the case files digitally, so the records were *huge*, taking up an increasing amount of space in my bedroom. I even had to get a file cabinet, which really clashed with my aesthetic.

I would read the record and write my brief based on the supervisor's suggestions. Then I would send my supervisor a draft and he or she would tell me it was formally sloppy but rhetorically strong. Then I would rewrite it and file the case, and I would normally lose. But because the appeals courts were so slow, by the time the opinion came out informing me that I'd lost, I didn't even remember what the case was about. I never invested much in winning or losing. I was like a macabre iteration of the soccer mom who "just hopes both teams have fun."

The weird thing was I never really spoke to my clients. My supervisors encouraged me to call them or write letters, but it was hard to reach them.

Eventually, I stopped even trying. I simply crafted their defenses based on the trial record and tried my best. I don't remember exactly how many cases I wrote; the details blended together. A lot of unconstitutional searches of Black and brown people that the appellate court maintained were A-OK.

I had neither hope nor faith in the system. This was just something to do. A way to pay rent.

In other words, for me, the stakes were low.

But I did feel more invested with my juvenile clients. I'd always wanted to work with juveniles because it felt like there was more opportunity to make a difference. That is, *any* opportunity to make a difference. If you can keep a juvenile out of prison, you can save their life. Prisons create criminals, triggering a cycle that's hard to break.

———

My first juvenile client was named Sierra, a redhead from Northern California I represented twice. First, for hitting a cop with a shoe (battery of a police officer). Second, for vehicle theft. (Get you a girl who can do both!)

I lost both cases.

Sierra was a victim of human trafficking, which made it all extra sad. She came from a broken and abusive home, rendering her more vulnerable to being trafficked. I googled her name and found her Twitter profile. Her bio was just the sparkle emoji; her profile picture depicted half of her face, sticking out her tongue. A normal-looking teen. There was only one tweet.

> set it off in this bitch lets go, bitch i aint friendly ion fuck with
> these hoes

In 2016, the same year as that tweet, Sierra's dad called the police regarding a family disturbance at his home. I knew this just from reading the cold record in my bedroom, not from meeting or talking to any of these people. (People always want to hear my courtroom stories, but I don't have any. There was a lingering possibility that I would have to present an oral argument—when the appeals court found it hard to decide— but that never happened to me.)

According to the record, Sierra's dad told the police that Sierra had become belligerent after he confiscated her cell phone. He called Sierra's mom to pick her up but needed help in the meantime.

When they arrived, the officers instructed Sierra to remain outside her house until her mom got there, to avoid another altercation. At one point, Sierra told the officer she wanted to sit on the porch and started walking across the lawn. The officer grabbed her arm to stop her and, as I phrased it in the brief, "a tennis shoe Sierra was holding hit him on the cheek."

After reading the record, I sat at my desk and started writing. I felt energized by the record, eager to advocate for this young woman, a clear victim of her circumstances and her teenage hormones. As I wrote, I forgot about everything I hated about the law and leaned into my comfort zone—crafting arguments. I thought of a Susan Sontag quote: "I'm now writing out of rage—and I feel a kind of Nietzschean elation. It's tonic. . . . I want to denounce everybody, tell everybody off. I go to my typewriter as I might go to my machine gun."[1]

I argued that the evidence presented at Sierra's juvenile hearing was insufficient to show she violated California Penal Code section 243, subdivision (b), battery of a police officer.

First, the officer was not acting in lawful performance of his duties when he grabbed a fifteen-year-old girl from behind without warning. Because the officer lacked reasonable suspicion that criminal activity was afoot—no pun intended—he exceeded the scope of his police duties and acted with unnecessary force when he grabbed her. Moreover, Sierra was erroneously found guilty because her behavior toward the officer was inadvertent rather than willful, and the state must prove purposeful conduct to prove battery. I argued the record showed the young girl reflexively flung her arm, which was carrying a shoe, in response to being grabbed unlawfully by the officer. Thus, the prosecution did not meet its burden to prove Sierra's guilt beyond a reasonable doubt.

The court didn't buy it.

Regarding my first argument, the court held that substantial evidence supported the juvenile court's finding that the use of force was reasonable in light of Sierra's resistance, and also supported the juvenile court's finding that the officer was lawfully performing his duties when he detained Sierra.

Regarding my second argument, the court held the juvenile court could "reasonably infer" that Sierra intentionally flung her arm at the cop. Obviously, the appellate judges had never been teenage girls. Our bodies were always doing things without warning!

The appeals court never went into too much detail, especially not in an unpublished opinion, which this was.

The second time I represented Sierra, she was challenging the denial of her Penal Code section 236.14 motion for vacatur—essentially, a motion to vacate a prior judgment. Sierra had been arrested a few more times in the interim, and Penal Code section 236.14 permits vacatur for a person arrested for or convicted of any nonviolent offense committed while he or she was a victim of human trafficking.

Again, I went to my keyboard and began typing with intensity, especially because I had failed her the first time.

I argued that Sierra's case was precisely the kind of situation that the legislature sought to address when creating section 236.14. As a child, Sierra had suffered domestic violence, neglect, trauma, and abuse, rendering her uniquely vulnerable to sex trafficking. The trafficking started as early as age twelve. The offenses Sierra sought to vacate—theft of a relative's car and fleeing from her group home—were nonviolent and were a direct result of her being trafficked, intertwined with her fractured family relationships. There was also a presumption of such given that there was official documentation of the trafficking. Sierra expressed a desire to leave human trafficking and to live a normal teenage life. The court's failure to exercise discretion mandated by law, I argued, constituted a violation of due process.

Again, the court disagreed, concluding: "The court was well within its discretion to deny Sierra's petition based on her failure to provide clear and convincing evidence the offenses were the direct result of her status as a human trafficking victim."

Bullshit! Of course her crimes were a result of human trafficking. Sierra was the reason this statute existed. She was like the fucking poster child for section 236.14. How could the court not see it? Were they just overworked? Lazy? Bored? Sociopathic?

When I looked at Sierra's Twitter profile recently, a new tweet had appeared. It is a link to a news story entitled "Teen Trafficked in Vegas, Chicago, Atlanta, Miami. Now She'll Return Home—to Fresno."

The story is about her.

———

Another client that stuck with me was a juvenile named Mori.

Her case was devastating.

Mori was thirteen when she was found guilty, with one count of being a minor in possession of tear gas—she pepper-sprayed a classmate—and put on probation. She didn't get jail time, thank god, but the fact that she was punished at all felt unjust.

Mori was walking home from school with her cousins when the victim started taunting her. He knew that her mother had passed away when Mori was very young. The victim made fun of Mori's clothes, and then said, "At least I don't suck dick" and "your mom is dead."

Reading this, I felt sick.

I even held back tears, which, as we know, are a rare experience for me.

After the victim made the comment about her mother, Mori sprayed him with pepper spray in the back of the head and in his face. She was remorseful for what she did and told police that, in retrospect, she could have handled the situation differently, but when the victim brought up her mother, her anger got the best of her and she reacted.

After her mom had died, Mori lived with her grandfather. Her grandfather had originally given her the pepper spray to protect herself because they lived in a bad neighborhood and Mori had been jumped the previous year.

My argument centered around California's established presumption that "a minor under the age of 14 is incapable of committing a crime." To defeat this presumption, the prosecution must show by "clear proof" that at the time the minor committed the charged act, he or she knew of its wrongfulness. But at the jurisdictional hearing, the prosecution made no attempt to establish that Mori—a thirteen-year-old—knew that her conduct was wrong.

I felt more strongly about Mori's case than any other case I worked on. Forming logical arguments on her behalf felt invigorating and cathartic. I was actually using my bitchiness for good. In fact, my bitchiness was rendered heroic.

In my brief, I stressed that Mori lost her mother at the age of six, last saw her father at nine, and was under the care of her grandfather, who had been accused of neglecting her multiple times. Put simply, Mori had dealt with a lot of trauma. And the catalyst for Mori's criminal behavior was her classmate picking at this very trauma, provoking her with "your mom is dead."

I reiterated trial counsel's argument that some really sensitive issues were triggered for her. Given that Mori was an emotionally disturbed thirteen-year-old, the court should have first determined whether Mori knew the conduct was wrong before declaring wardship and imposing formal probation.

When I read the court's opinion, I cried:

[Minor] appeals from the juvenile court's orders declaring her a ward of the court and placing her on formal probation following her no-contest plea to a misdemeanor violation of Penal Code section 22810, subdivision (d), possession of tear gas by a minor. [Minor] was 13 years old at the time. She argues the wardship finding and probation order must be set aside because the district attorney did not prove, the court did not find, and the record does not support an implied finding that she knew the wrongfulness of her conduct at the time of its commission. We agree. We therefore reverse and remand for further proceedings.

I won!

I got that druggy feeling I had when I won my first case at the San Francisco Public Defender. That high of validation and reward. I was being told by the state that I was right and it was wrong. But this time was even better. Because that former DUI client had been guilty—he was drunk-driving—but I believed Mori's behavior was justified. She was just thirteen, and an adjudication on her record could change the course of her entire life. I might have saved her. I probably didn't, but I might have. I have no idea where she is now, but for those few seconds I felt a glimmer of hope.

Mori's case was the only case I won and actually expected to win. The other times I won felt more like situations when the court wanted to make a new rule of law and my case just happened to contain the facts it needed to do that. My wins certainly weren't based on the strength of my argumentation.

Curtis's case was a perfect example.

Curtis was pulled over for false registration tabs in Napa. Another officer arrived at the scene after he heard Curtis's name over the police radio and recognized him from a domestic violence report from the day before.

When the second officer arrived, he told the first officer that there was probable cause to arrest Curtis for the DV incident. So he asked Curtis to get out of the car and handcuffed him. After Curtis was placed in the cop car, the officer went back to Curtis's car and found a baton.

Curtis was charged with felony weapon possession. As with the vast majority of my appeals, I challenged the search that revealed the contraband on Fourth Amendment grounds. Basically, the Fourth Amendment requires that a police officer's search be backed by a warrant absent certain exceptions. I argued that none of those exceptions were present here.

I didn't feel particularly strongly about my argument.

In my brief I wrote that the search incident to arrest exception did not apply because there was no suggestion that evidence of the crime of arrest—a domestic dispute—would be found in his vehicle. I argued the plain view exception did not apply because the officer did not discover the baton from a lawful vantage point. I argued the search could not be justified by the inventory search exception because there was no evidence the car was inventoried. And, finally, the inevitable discovery doctrine did not apply because the prosecution did not prove that, in the event the baton was not illegally seized on the scene, the baton would have inevitably been discovered by valid protocol.

The First District Court of Appeal agreed that there was no substantial evidence that the officer conducted an inventory search, and there was no substantial evidence that the police inevitably would have discovered the baton.

But I was annoyed they didn't quote me at all in the decision.

Curtis called me on the phone. He was thrilled. This was the only time I spoke to a client on the phone. Mori's grandfather called me a lot and I got a few letters from jail, but mostly my appellate clients were invisible to me.

"We've made history," Curtis said.

I guess for you, I thought.

———

I didn't feel like I was making history.

Appellate law mostly involved sitting at a desk alone crafting arguments for people. To entertain myself during the dry legal research portion of the job, I started a Twitter account called

"Law Without Context" (@born2judge), where I'd post snippets of cases, well, without context. Judges can be very salty and hilarious. Sometimes on purpose, like:

> law without context
> @born2judge
>
> .
>
> Feb 23, 2017
> I am so perplexed by the way the law applicable to this case
> has developed that it would be inappropriate for me to try

And sometimes not on purpose, like:

> law without context
> @born2judge
>
> .
>
> Sep 26, 2017
> the Bentley was constitutionally material

And often hearing criminal activity discussed in dry, legal terms is just hysterical. For example:

> law without context
> @born2judge
>
> .
>
> Mar 21, 2018
> While waiting to take the breathalyzer test, defendant stated
> something like "that Dayquil will mess you up."

Or:

law without context

@born2judge

.

Nov 22, 2017

gang members feel no loyalty to a hood rat who parties with them

Finding these snippets and posting them on Twitter made the research more fun and gave me a creative project.

To be honest, I never really read entire cases or records. I mostly skimmed them for what I needed, just like I did all throughout law school. I took advantage of the digital tools I had at my disposal, ones not available to people like my dad who started practicing law before the internet was invented. I used a healthy combination of Ctrl+F, the search key in MS Word, and the chat function on the legal search engine Lexis to find what I needed.

Say, for example, my client was charged with possession of meth, and the cops exceeded the lawful scope of search incident to probation when they searched my client's makeup bag, where they found the meth. I would use the chat function and ask the Lexis minions to craft a search to yield cases where courts in my jurisdiction found the cops exceeded the scope of a lawful probation search when they searched a bag that the defendant had never been seen holding.

They would come up with something crazy-looking, like: "Exceed!" W/ 10 ("scope" AND "search").

I don't know what it means either! But for some reason that's how you find the cases, and I would have no idea how to do that on my own. I would just copy and paste whatever they said into the search box, then skim the resulting cases for the language I needed.

I asked a few of my lawyer friends if they used the Lexis minions, but none of them even knew the chat function was a thing. I was shocked my friends were able to craft these crazy search terms themselves.

Lawyers have a lot of pride, but I am the most shameless bitch on the planet.

Anyway, I'd use the freaky search terms the Lexis minions told me to use (some minions were better than others). Then I'd click on each case and Ctrl+F the fuck out of it. Instead of reading the cases, I would just look for the sentence I needed, a sentence like: "The officer exceeded the scope of a lawful probation search when he searched a bag outside of defendant's dominion or control."

Then I would compare the facts of the cases. If the court held for the defendant, I would argue that the facts of that case and the facts of my case were, like, *identical.* If the court held for the state, I would say the facts of that case were absolutely nothing like the facts of mine.

It was fun! I was being paid by the government to tell the government it was wrong, which for an irreverent provocatrice like *moi* was a small slice of heaven.

I used the Lexis Advance account of a girl I'd gone on one date with when I first moved to LA. We didn't have any romantic chemistry, but we got along well as friends. Like me, she was an overprivileged blonde lesbian addicted to collecting degrees as a way to avoid real-world responsibility. She already had an MBA and was currently getting her JD. She joked that she was going to go to med school next. She grew up in Beverly Hills, and I worried that we looked alike.

We met at a cocktail bar on the east side. She chain-smoked cigarettes and wore a lighter around her neck on a necklace. She had no idea where her car was, and told me she was nervous about the 3L writing requirement—she had to write a big paper and writing wasn't her thing.

I told her I was good at writing law school papers if she needed help.

We never went on another date, but she did take me up on my offer to help her with her paper. The next year, she sent me a lot of chaotic, amphetamine-induced emails filled with snippets of research, and she paid me $1K to turn it into a paper.

I was *furious* when she got an A–. She was happy, but I wasn't. She went to a mediocre law school and I'd gone to Berkeley! I would have taken the paper more seriously if my name was on it, I told myself. Also, she did all the research. Plus I wrote it very quickly.

But at least I got her Lexis password.

The research and writing have always been fun for me, but formatting continued to be my bête noire. Unlike the judges, my appellate supervisors cared *a lot* about formatting. I never met them, but I talked to them on the phone when they made me. They mostly sent me condescending emails. I imagined them all as former debate-club nerds in polo shirts and pleated khakis, clinging hard to their ability to follow inane rules as their sole way to hold power over others.

My female supervisors were particularly scathing. This is something I'd noticed at other law jobs as well. Women had been excluded from practicing the law until relatively recently; there was only one woman in my dad's graduating law school class. In other words, whenever I was supervised by an older female lawyer, I knew she had gone through serious obstacles to get to where she was. And she was generally irked as hell by my entitled punk ass, which—to be fair—was very understandable.

My male supervisors could be scathing, too, in different ways and for different reasons. My female supervisors were curt; they had no time for me, and I respected that. The men were nerds who seemed to enjoy being condescending for sport, almost like a flirt, or to overcompensate for some deep-seated inadequacy. They all reminded me of my law school boyfriend Charlie.

One time, my supervisor (David, I'm sure, because one-third of all lawyers are named David) emailed me: "Do you want to know what the worst sentence in your brief was?"

I wanted to respond, "Are you telling me you didn't have sex until you were thirty-five? Because that is what I am hearing."

That said, sometimes I am nostalgic for the sassy and blunt way lawyers speak to each other. Later, when I got a job at a start-up, people were always trying to engage in mind-numbing small talk, like what my weekend plans were and which TV shows I watched. Their attempts to "get to know me" felt inefficient and pointless. I wasn't looking for friends. I was there for a paycheck.

And then there were the court clerks, who were real pieces of work. I mean, I guess they were just doing their job. Pretty much every time I filed a brief, which I did online, the clerks rejected it for some reason or another. The indents were the wrong size. The page numbers were on the wrong part of the page. I forgot to bookmark the headings. They were not fucking around with formatting rules. Not at all.

Sometimes I wasn't made aware of the mistake until after

the deadline for my brief—government workers move like molasses—which meant I would have to petition the court to forgive me for missing the deadline and allow me to refile the brief.

One time I was so pissed off the court rejected another one of my briefs and I slammed my laptop hard enough to frighten a nearby family at LAX—several of them *jumped*. The California government always focused on the wrong things. It was 2019. Why did they need a hard copy? Surely, the Court of Appeal had printers. Why did they need page numbers? Why waste my fucking time? Why waste everyone's time? People's liberty was at stake!

But looking back, I think of it as a pretty chill job.

I used my personal Gmail with Bubbles the Powerpuff Girl as my icon, which certainly would not have flown at a law firm. Working for the government is nice because, again, it's *super* slow, no one is ever on your ass. The things I hated about it are mostly things I hate about having a job in general: I don't like being told what to do. I don't like having to follow rules I didn't create for myself. And I didn't feel like I was making a positive contribution to society. Even with the cases I won, my clients were all beyond fucked and there was nothing I could do to change that.

I thought my client was innocent only one time.

Before everyone knew about how bad the criminal justice system was—basically, before Ava DuVernay's indictment of the prison-industrial complex *13th* came out on Netflix—I'd get raised eyebrows when I told people I represented criminals. I'd try to justify it and they would throw me a bone and say, "Well, I'm sure a lot of people are wrongfully accused." I'd just nod, not wanting to go into it.

It's very hard for me to talk about the criminal justice system in a social setting. My blood starts to boil. People are wrongfully accused sometimes, sure, but it's much more complicated than that.

The criminal justice system tends to be a vehicle to enforce social stratification. We put poor people and people of color and mentally ill people in front of a jury and call them bad eggs without acknowledging that we failed to give them adequate education and social services and the tools they needed to survive. So they steal something or join a gang, for survival, and then we lock them up, with more criminals, where they learn to be better criminals, and they are released as felons and have no hope of getting a job, and they're stuck in the prison-industrial complex forever.

While I was writing a second draft of this book, a man named George Floyd was killed by a Minneapolis police officer for allegedly using a counterfeit bill. The officer knelt on Floyd's neck for almost nine minutes, cutting off his air supply. Videos of the gruesome killing circulated, and riots broke out across the country. The Black Lives Matter movement was reinvigorated, and indignation over the carceral state seeped into the popular consciousness.

Floyd's death did not shock me, having worked in criminal defense. But I was glad people were finally paying attention. The same people who were once shocked that I "defended criminals" were now posting heated calls to "defund the police."

Something had shifted, and I felt a glimmer of hope. People were waking up.

As author Sarah Schulman put it so perfectly in her book *Conflict Is Not Abuse*: "The law is designed to protect the state, not people who are victimized by the state."[2]

So, yes, my clients were mostly "guilty," technically, under the elements of the statutes. But we, as a society, pushed them there.

That said, I'll never forget the one time I thought my client was innocent.

It was another juvenile case. Jared was charged with felony attempted robbery. The incident occurred one evening in San Jose. I still have trouble picturing exactly what went down. This is one hard thing about criminal defense. Both sides build pictures of the crime scene based on what the defendant, victim, and witnesses said happened. But memory is imperfect, especially in the heightened emotional circumstances of a violent crime.

On appeal, it's even harder to picture what happened. I was working off cold records. Again, I rarely ever talked to my clients. I never spoke with Jared. I simply read the transcript and tried my best to picture what had happened.

The alleged victim, Kayla, testified that she was walking home from the subway station when her dad, Franklin, called her on the phone. He said he was about to stop at their home to pick up his work ID. Kayla noticed two boys near her. She stayed on the phone with Franklin.

When Kayla went to unlock the front gate of her house, the two boys she had noticed earlier were on either side of her. One of them said, "Run your shit," and then lifted his shirt, revealing a handgun. Kayla punched him, then the other person tried to pin her to the ground. They tried to take her phone and wallet, but they couldn't. Eventually, they gave up and ran away.

Franklin testified that after he picked up his ID, still on the phone with Kayla and driving by the house, he saw three men near his daughter. After he heard what was happening over the phone, he made a U-turn. He saw my client, Jared, alone, running across the street.

Franklin didn't see any part of the attempted robbery, but he assumed Jared was involved because Jared came from the direction of the house and was running.

Franklin then chased Jared in his car, yelling, "Stop. I got you."

Jared kept running. Eventually, he dove into a laundromat and locked himself in the bathroom.

Franklin followed Jared into the laundromat. He banged on the bathroom door and threatened Jared until the police arrived.

Kayla went to the laundromat and identified Jared as one of her attackers.

I know, I know. I know how it sounds.

But I believe Jared's account.

Jared testified that as soon as he realized his friends were going to rob Kayla, he ran away because he did not want to be involved.

I was moved by Jared's account saying that he didn't want to be involved in the robbery. So much of juvenile crime is about peer pressure. It took a lot of courage for Jared to ditch his friends. And the fact that he was punished for doing the right thing, simply because he was the first person Franklin saw, felt deeply unfair.

I pictured him locked in the laundromat bathroom with

Franklin trying to bang down the door, and how scary that must have been.

Of course, Jared could have been lying. But my gut said he was telling the truth. Especially because Franklin saw three people and Kayla said she had only two attackers.

But even if Jared was lying, from a legal perspective, the evidence didn't prove his guilt beyond a reasonable doubt. Then again, the evidence almost *never* proves guilt beyond a reasonable doubt. And despite this, roughly 75 percent of criminal trials in the United States end in conviction.[3]

Aside from arguing that the record lacked substantial evidence showing Jared committed the robbery, I also argued that Kayla's identification was erroneously admitted and that the juvenile court improperly excluded expert testimony. I won't get into those arguments because they're dry, but the court bought none of it.

This broke my heart.

The appeals court did not address my substantial evidence argument other than to say: "The in-field identification was reliable under the totality of the circumstances and, contrary to the minor's argument on appeal, constitutes substantial evidence of guilt."

Conviction affirmed.

CHAPTER 15

Representing a Rapist

This incident began as "normal teenage behavior."

That was how the probation report put it. My client, a seventeen-year-old named Tyler, was charged and convicted of California Penal Code section 269, subdivision (a)(2): rape by force, violence, duress, menace, or fear. I was appointed to represent him on appeal.

My friends were shocked to hear that I—at that point a *proud feminist* and low-key misandrist—was representing a convicted rapist. They were even more surprised to learn that I was able to do so without feeling compromised.

"So, he's innocent?" they'd ask.

"No," I'd say. Again, my clients were *rarely* innocent. And what is "innocent" anyway? Sex crimes are complex.

And I wasn't arguing that he was innocent but rather that he—a teen—should be given sex-offender treatment instead of incarceration.

Tyler met his victim at the mall, where both he and his mom worked. He saw the victim, whom he recognized from school, and struck up a conversation. They flirted in typical teenage fashion, strolling around and discussing their mutual interests—music and TV and whatever else teens are into . . . TikTok? My client wanted to put his new iPad in his mom's car, so the teens retrieved the mom's keys and went to the parking lot. In the car, they began making out.

Their accounts of what happened next differed drastically, and, as in most sex crimes, there were no other witnesses to confirm or deny either account. My client maintains the victim said yes through her actions, then no through equivocation, then yes with her actions again. Afterward, the two walked back to the mall together and followed each other on Instagram. They continued to direct message each other after the incident and the messages were friendly.

It was not until months later, when an officer came to his school asking to speak with him, that my client understood that what he did was wrong. At the time of his juvenile court proceedings, he was incredibly remorseful and ashamed. Both his current girlfriend and ex-girlfriend testified that he had never pressured them sexually; in fact, they'd never even had sex. His probation officer testified that because he would have a strike against him for the rest of his life and a juvenile sex offense on his record (ineligible to be sealed), his lifelong dream of being a nurse was "gone."

I thought it was wildly unfair. I mean, think of your first sexual experience. Did you know what you were doing? I certainly didn't.

My law school friend Lara, who has worked on a number of rape and sexual assault cases, recalled a similar story. She told me about a client who was charged with sexually assaulting a child. On the day of the incident, she said, "no one, including the adult witnesses, thought anything untoward had occurred." Over time, however, stories "changed and became more and more deviant."

Lara told me that "the criminal justice system is poorly equipped for all sex crimes, but especially those with any subtlety." She said that if a friend of hers was ever raped and did not get a rape kit done at the hospital ASAP, "I don't know if I could advise her to report the crime to the police, because the system traumatizes people; it does not work to make them whole."

Less than a year after this conversation, Lara was raped at a work party and reported it to the police. The subsequent criminal proceedings became a smut campaign in which she was painted as a sexually aggressive femme fatale. It was all too traumatizing; she eventually asked the DA to drop the case.

The United States is among the most punitive nations in the world. When it comes to sex-related offenses, we are uniquely draconian. The average time served for rape is sixty months in the United States, compared to thirty-four months on average in our peer countries. And all fifty states have enacted sex-offender-registration statutes, which require a wide array of offenders to register or otherwise be criminalized. Today, convicted sex offenders—ranging from rapists and pedophiles to young people in consensual relationships to public urinators and indecent exposures—are forced to live under highways and in encampments.[1]

And as with most feminist issues and nearly all aspects of the criminal justice system, there is also a troubling racial element at play.

Scholars show that rape convictions disproportionately target

Black men and leave Black women without redress.[2] While cold cases continue to go stale in inner cities, resolute prosecutors throw the book at the defendant when the complaining witness is credible or, a cynic, or perhaps a realist, would say, when the witness is white. As with most other crimes, vulnerable populations—people of color, women, people with disabilities—continue to be disproportionately affected by these biases. Citing Michelle Alexander, Lara told me that the prison-industrial complex continues "to rely on the free labor of black and brown people."[3]

I often think that our hysteria-driven, hyper-punitive response to the broad category of those we call "sex offenders" is ineffective and counterproductive. And I worry that in focusing all of our attention on harshly punishing the "evil" perpetrators, we might be missing the root of the issue: our collective societal failure to properly educate both men and women on appropriate and consensual sexual behavior.

It didn't seem fair that my teenage client's life was going to be ruined because he misread signals that likely no one had taught him to read in the first place.

Most of us get "the talk," but we rarely are taught to be clear with our intentions. In the media—at least when I was growing up in the nineties—men were portrayed as the sexual initiators and women as their coy prey. The men would push for sex and the women would giggle "no" until the men eventually got their way. Not only was this how sex "went," but also we were told it was "hot." Women are told our pussies should be "tight," but the only reason a vagina is tight is because the woman is scared—our vaginal canals contract with fear and this turns men on. Porn takes it further by normalizing brutality, which is why my feminist icon Kitty MacKinnon crusaded so fiercely against it. Hence her iconic quote: "Man fucks woman; subject verb object."[4]

In every one of the demeaning and nonconsensual sexual situations I've been in personally, a small part of me has been turned on.

I don't think this is because I'm broken. I actually think it's pretty normal. I was socialized as a woman. As Chimamanda Ngozi Adichie explained in her viral TED Talk, famously co-opted by Beyoncé: "We teach women to shrink themselves."[5]

Once, a man at a party asked if there was a female equivalent to men comparing their dick sizes.

I laughed. *Imagine every single thing about you is your dick*, I thought. *And instead of big, it has to be as small as possible.*

And one of the main things that we need to be small is our sexual desire.

The fuzzy line between normal intercourse and criminal sex in a patriarchal society partially explains why, in many cases, neither party realizes anything was out of the ordinary at the time the sex act occurred.

I was working on Tyler's case when my social media feeds exploded with the #MeToo movement. A part of me was happy to watch the masses cling to feminism. But as a criminal defense attorney representing a convicted rapist who, in my view, deserved sympathy rather than scorn, I was turned off by the movement's vindictive response to sex crimes. The feminism on my timeline was reductive. It was black and white. *Men are trash! Women are queens! Kill all men! BELIEVE ALL WOMEN!*

Well, women are humans, too. We abuse power when it's given to us, and we lie or bend the truth for self-preservation. As a society, we can't just nakedly believe all women and kill all men. Men are victims, too, of a culture that fails to properly teach all genders about consensual sex.

Contemporary mainstream feminism points fingers and screams moral absolutisms without any understanding of how the power structures in which we are all complicit work to enable oppressive behavior.

Sexual assault is a systemic issue that has much more to do with society and power than it has to do with individual "bad actors," or men in general. Women can also abuse our power. The first person to slap me across the face in the bedroom was a woman. I've had as many nonconsensual sexual encounters with women as I have had with men. This makes sense because gay women tend to mimic heteronormative patterns— that is our model, and such behavior is typically rewarded. But I've noticed that women can get away with more womanizing behavior because we are less policed. Plenty of influential women abuse their power and prey on vulnerable women in the manner of Harvey Weinstein, but do we hear about it? No. Because society doesn't respect women enough to see us as capable of sexual predation. The only role we are entitled to play is the victim; this is the role we've *always* played. And #MeToo is just another iteration of that.

I agree with law professor Elizabeth Schneider's argument that feminism should "learn to accept contradiction, ambiguity, and ambivalence in women's lives, and explore more 'grays' in our conceptions of women's experience."[6]

Beyoncé has always been among my favorite feminists for this reason. The same album that features Chimamanda Ngozi Adichie's iconic feminist TED Talk contains a reference to Ike Turner forcing cake into Tina Turner's mouth, an implicit glorification of domestic violence. But there is an honesty and authenticity to the fact that Bey's feminism is constantly being contradicted and renegotiated. It also calls into question the prevailing ideology: *Radio says speed it up, I just go slower.*

———

In 2018, a *Buzzfeed* journalist named Jakob emailed me after I reviewed Tao Lin's book *Trip*—a memoir about healing through psychedelics—for the *Los Angeles Review of Books*. Jakob said he was writing about "Tao Lin's return to publishing with *Trip* after statutory and relationship abuse allegations were brought against him in 2014."

He asked, "Were you aware of the allegations against him when you decided to review the book? If so, what are your thoughts on the role journalists, reviewers, and interviewers should play when writing about work by artists accused of abuse? I'm especially curious about how that might interact with your role as a lawyer."

The email infuriated me. I've been a devout Tao fan since 2013 when I bought his novel *Taipei* in a Berkeley bookstore because the glittery cover was so beautiful. (I firmly believe you *can* judge a book by its cover.) I read the book slowly to savor it. It felt so fresh, with sentences seemingly plucked from real life, like "Paul asked if he liked Rilo Kiley and he became quiet for a few seconds, seeming worried, like he might not be able to answer, before saying, 'um, not really.' "[7]

I was sick of plotty mysteries with fatal consequences that felt nothing like actual life. In *Taipei*, nothing really happens. A fictionalized Tao and his fictionalized wife float around readings and parties and libraries and take drugs. I guess the stakes are that they could have died. Other than that, the conflict is mostly within the confines of their relationship. I loved how Tao captures the dull malaise of contemporary life. How monotony breeds self-destruction. I loved how his protagonist is equal parts off-putting and endearing, how he struggles with social interaction and feels imprisoned by his insecurity.

Honestly, it reminded me of the female experience.

When Jakob came for Tao, my criminal defense brain immediately went into overdrive. Tao was misunderstood and I would defend him. I composed a heated response, which I blamed on my brunchtime Bloody Mary, but really it's just my personality. If anything, the alcohol tempered me. I wrote:

> I was aware of the statutory rape allegations, and I know that Tao maintained that their sex was consensual and legal (given the age of consent in Pennsylvania). I am also aware that Kennedy [his alleged victim] deleted the allegations, and asked Jezebel to take down the article announcing them, stating: "i shouldn't have started this im trying to recover from a [psychiatric] hospitalization."

> Either way, I am more concerned with Tao's value as an artist than his guilt or innocence. I do not view him or his work as perpetuating toxic masculinity. The job of an artist is to confront uncomfortable truths. Tao's work grapples with the gravity of male oppression, rather than buries it under clichéd accounts of implausible romance. In Richard Yates, which fictionalizes his relationship with Kennedy, Tao's protagonist

struggles with his own internalized misogyny. Trip, published 8 years later, finds the author in a very different place: he's celibate and "trend[ing] toward the feminine."

The patriarchy is not upheld by a few isolated bad acts; rather it is a system of oppression in which we are all complicit. The most important task in dismantling the patriarchy is to honestly acknowledge and engage with our own complicity. If journalists are interested in combating toxic masculinity, they should focus more on elevating stories about female desire and autonomy, and less on narratives in which women need "good men" to save them or make them whole.

I'm not sure if he picked up on the fact that the last sentence was directed at him. Put simply, women don't need a "good man" like him to protect us from "bad men" like Tao Lin via think pieces in *Buzzfeed*. Instead, maybe cover a book written by a woman. Or listen to a woman next time she tries to tell you how she feels.

At the time, I glossed over the detail that this *Buzzfeed* journalist had asked about how my reviewing the book "might interact with [my] role as a lawyer." But looking back, I might say that criminal defense goes hand in hand with feminism in that it questions the power of the state, which, as we all know, is run by men.

Regardless of my oversight, my defense of Tao was heavily cited in the article. Afterward, Tao emailed me.

The subject line said "Thank you" and the email simply said:

Hi Anna, Thank you for your thoughts in the Buzzfeed article.

A bit starstruck, I emailed him and linked an early version of this chapter—a Medium essay. He replied. His response included the following piece of encouragement:

> I feel like your piece would make a good book, or an essay in a collection, are you working on a book?

Well, it was this email that inspired me to write the book proposal for *Bad Lawyer*. It was the alleged statutory rapist who gave me the courage to write this book, my debut memoir. In doing so, Tao was fulfilling the very role I told Jakob men *should* fulfill: encouraging women to tell their own stories, instead of stepping in to do it for them.

In embracing a black-and-white, reductive, and merciless response to sex crimes, we miss these sorts of opportunities for men to be good, to learn from their mistakes.

My teenage client was denied a chance to be good.

I lost my case.

CHAPTER 16

Horny for the Law

One night while drunk at a party, I pitched writing a column about feminism and the criminal justice system.

Honestly, I had no memory of doing this until the editor emailed me the next week, saying she was excited about my column. She decided to call it "All Rise" and would be paying me $450 per article (!).

This was more than I'd ever made writing. Previously, I'd been writing for a music blog, making just a hundred dollars per article. Being a music blogger felt kind of embarrassing at age thirty. Especially because I had a law degree.

I wanted to write about other things.

More than that, I wanted to be taken seriously.

I wrote my first "All Rise" article about Michelle Carter, the modelesque twenty-year-old from small-town Massachusetts who was convicted of manslaughter for "convincing" her boyfriend to commit suicide. After meeting in Florida on vacation, Michelle and her alleged victim, Conrad, struck up a mostly digital romance, exchanging more than twenty thousand text messages over the course of several years. The romance ended in July 2014, when Conrad poisoned himself with carbon dioxide fumes in a Kmart parking lot.

This was his second suicide attempt.

Michelle, who was seventeen when Conrad died, had repeatedly encouraged her boyfriend to get professional help over the course of their relationship. A few days before his suicide, however, Michelle changed her tune. You're gonna have to prove me wrong, she texted him, because I just don't think you really want this. You just keep pushing it off to another night and say you'll do it but you never do.

At one point during the attempt, Conrad got out of the car filled with deadly fumes and called Michelle, who told him to get back in the car. The judge found this phone call sufficient to constitute homicide, and Michelle was sentenced to two and a half years in prison.

I was obsessed with the case. The legal issues were novel: Can someone be convicted of homicide for their words alone? But more than that, I was fascinated by the narratives spun around Michelle and the public vitriol directed toward her.

The case reeked of misogyny, as most criminal trials do.

In her opening statement, the district attorney said Michelle was "desperate for attention and sympathy from classmates" and used Conrad as a "pawn in her sick game of life and death." Patriarchs have cast women as attention-seeking and manipulative since the beginning of time, and these descriptions therefore always give me pause. They should give everyone pause.

But the public—even those who believed Michelle was wrongfully convicted of homicide—quickly latched on to the prosecutor's narrative.

An attorney friend of mine texted me: She deserved it, but I'm concerned with the precedent.

Why did she deserve it? I asked.

She was preying on someone mentally and emotionally unstable.

He then compared Michelle to Lady Macbeth.

To me, the facts suggest a more nuanced situation. At trial, Michelle's treating psychiatrist testified that she was a vulnerable person who wanted desperately to help end the suffering of the boyfriend she loved. Her efforts don't seem radically different from someone helping a terminally ill loved one end his or her life.

The article I wrote for "All Rise" generated some traffic, and I felt like I was finally finding my beat. For the first time, I felt like I was writing about something people seemed to care about.

I wrote my next "All Rise" article about Alissa Nutting's novel *Tampa*—written from the perspective of a sexy female pedophile—and our societal failure to see women as sexual predators, and why it mattered. In it, I explored whether society is willing to punish sexual misconduct when the defendant is a conventionally attractive woman. Doesn't every teenage boy fantasize about having sex with his hot blonde teacher?

I also wrote about courtroom sexism, inspired by Sarah Paulson's portrayal of Marcia Clark in Ryan Murphy's *The People v. OJ Simpson*. I wrote about defending rape cases as a feminist, portions of which you read in the last chapter. After the Harvey Weinstein scandal and explosion of the #MeToo movement, I wrote a primer on the law around workplace sexual harassment. After watching Molly in *Insecure*, I was inspired to write about how Big Law is still an ole boys' club, and interviewed a bunch of my lawyer friends about their lives in the golden handcuffs to do it.

Sometimes my articles were inspired by pop culture, and other times they just came to me while I was living my life.

That spring, I was out for drinks with friends at a bar in Silver Lake when we got an alarming text from another friend. There was an open shooter at Trader Joe's, just down the street. Gathered around a propped iPhone screen, we watched updates roll in on Twitter. It was a hostage situation. Videos appeared of police rescuing children from parked cars and people climbing out of the store's windows.

Eventually, a tweet announced that an innocent woman had been killed.

The vague way in which the tweet was worded made it clear to me that the woman was shot dead by the police.

The next day, my suspicions were confirmed. I read that the shooter began firing at police as he ran into the Trader Joe's. Two officers returned fire, and one bullet struck the deceased, a store employee, killing her instantly.

I also read that the incident began as a domestic violence situation at the shooter's home in South LA. The police were called, and—ultimately—an innocent woman was shot dead.

For "All Rise," I wrote about how calling the police often causes more harm than good—particularly in cases of domestic violence. In the wake of George Floyd's death, the masses woke up to how police can exacerbate rather than reduce violence, particularly when marginalized individuals are involved. But this wasn't common knowledge at that time. And with #MeToo raging, the average person didn't realize how dangerous a domestic violence report could be.

My thesis was that recent policy shifts toward a more punitive model in cases of domestic violence ignored the facts that law enforcement and the criminal justice system are often ill-equipped to protect women from abuse and, in many cases, only make it worse.

To vent my frustration with the adversarial system (I was still doing criminal appeals at the time), I wrote about restorative justice, which favors collaboration over combat and embraces more nuance than litigation does. As Michael, one of the main characters in *The Knockout Queen*, reflects: "I can see the human impulse to try to make the world look like it should, where bad people are punished and good people succeed, but, like, sometimes it seems very weird and childish to me."[1]

It *is* weird and childish. Revenge is a very primitive impulse. And it does nothing for the victims. In fact, restorative justice emerged in the seventies to combat the Western legal system's general neglect of victims and their needs.

Before long, I had thousands of followers on Medium.

People would comment about how much they liked my pieces. People would email me, too. It was crazy. A literary agent from ICM even reached out to me. She ghosted me not long after, but I still felt like I was getting somewhere. It was strange this was all happening from writing about *law*, the thing I'd been trying to escape, the thing I hated. But at the same time, I experienced a sort of ease writing about the law, especially in contrast to practicing it. I had achieved critical distance that felt necessary for my sanity. And I had all this content and all these strong feelings, which I suppose is the magic potion for writing something people want to read.

Also, I knew people fetishized the law. Beyond the procedural crime shows, legal shows like *The Good Wife*, *Suits*, *How to Get Away with Murder*, *The Practice*, *Goliath*, *Damages*, *Ally McBeal*—the list goes on—had or have huge followings. The most popular novels are legal thrillers by former lawyers such as John Grisham and Scott Turow. The most famous novel of all time, *To Kill a Mockingbird*, is about a rape trial.

Let's face it: people are horny for the law.

One day while coworking with some friends at a bar, I said I might try to turn "All Rise" into a book proposal. My friends seemed into it. We all agreed, people were obsessed with the law. This was shortly after the biergarten folly, and the title *Bad Lawyer* popped in my head.

If there was anything people fetishized more than the law, it was being bad at things.

"Get that money," my friend April said.

———

When I was about to hit my second anniversary as an appellate attorney, I was offered a position writing full-time for a start-up.

The company advertised itself as providing "thought leadership content." I had no idea what that meant. The CEO, a twenty-eight-year-old who had self-published a memoir about his teenage gaming addiction, reached out to me because of an essay I had written on Medium about loving the internet. The CEO, whose name was Jack Gold but who went by Gold because, well, *bros*, said the essay resonated with his own experience and he wanted to hire me. I wasn't exactly excited about this, given "thought leadership" sounded made up and Gold was the opposite of who I envisioned my audience to be. The job would require me to ghostwrite blog posts for entrepreneurs. As is likely clear at this point, there are few things I am less interested in than business. BUT. It was a full-time writing job. Salary. Benefits. And remote.

I could quit law.

I took the thought leadership job without much thought.

Not long after I started, I received a letter in the mail from the California Bar Association reminding me to pay my bar fees. I threw away the notice.

I threw away the subsequent notices as well.

Shortly after my final notice, Kim Kardashian announced she was taking the bar exam to become a criminal justice lawyer. Of all the Kardashian twists and turns, this one threw me for the biggest loop. Mostly because throughout law school and my legal career, I was way more interested in reality TV than I was in the Supreme Court or whatever. The law just always felt so tired and stilted. A good ole boys' club. A universe where things *are this way* because *they've been this way*, with insufficient awareness of how fucking problematic that rationale is in a country like the United States, where things have *been this way* mostly because of racism and sexism and classism, among many other bad *-isms*.

The law felt like the past, and the Kardashians were the future.

Throughout my dalliance with the law, I watched *Keeping Up* to unwind at night and escape my bleak fate in this male-dominated, blazered hellscape. And then, just as I'm leaving the law to become a writer (more on that shortly), Kim Kardashian tells *Vogue* she's taking the California Bar Exam. She's being mentored by two lawyers from San Francisco (where I practiced) and plans to do criminal justice work (my former field).

What the literal fuck!?

It all began when Kim learned via social media of Alice Marie Johnson, a sixty-three-year-old woman who'd been in an Alabama prison on a nonviolent drug charge since 1996. Kim was appalled that this grandmother received the same sentence as Charles Manson for a first-time nonviolent offense. She sent the story to her attorney and said, "What can we do?" A few months later, Kim convinced President Trump to grant Johnson clemency.[2]

I was as excited with this result as I was with Kanye's aesthetic revamp of the Kardashians.

Hollywood activism tends to feel performative and empty at best, counterproductive at worst. Celebrities throw garish galas and preach of equality, ignorant to the irony that they're draped in blood diamonds. They wear black on the red carpet and think it will solve the gender pay gap. Lavish charity galas frequently fail to raise more money than they cost to throw, or they barely break even.

Kim's effort felt heroic in comparison. She gave a woman her life back. Sure, you could say she did it for press. But she told *Vogue* it was actually the opposite—her publicist told her not to step foot in Trump's White House because it could ruin her career.

If there is a more valiant use of your celebrity than getting a person of color out of prison, I cannot think of one.

During the process, Kim was working with Van Jones and Jessica Jackson, cofounders of #cut50—a national bipartisan advocacy group for criminal justice reform.

I wrote about all of this for "All Rise."

At this point, my new novel, *Vagablonde*, was "on sub"—which I'd learned meant "on submission." I was beyond nervous. I couldn't mentally handle not selling a book again. I just couldn't.

I needed a project to preoccupy me. Luckily, I wasn't one of those people who can't work when anxious. I always hear of "paralyzing anxiety," but mine turns me into a machine. When my mind feels bleak, I figure I may as well get some shit done.

Writing always had a way of soothing my mind.

So many writers talk about the writing process as torturous, but to me writing is one of the only things in life that *isn't* torturous. Small talk? That's torturous. Taking my car to the mechanic? Torturous. Commercial air travel? Torturous. Filling out forms? Torturous. Writing? *Luxury*.

My coworkers at the start-up seemed really interested in "getting to know me," which made me nervous. They were all on Slack all day posting GIFs from *The Office* and asking me if I had any pets. Given my lack of participation, the HR person asked me if my Slack was working. I told her it was working fine.

Culturally, this environment couldn't be more different from that of my previous legal jobs. Lawyers do not ask you about your interests and most have no idea what a GIF is. They keep to themselves unless they need something from you. When they give you feedback, it's very direct and a little mean.

The start-up environment is very "supportive." They tell you you have *potential*. They sandwich constructive criticism in between effusive compliments. At my legal jobs, my writing was always "inappropriately casual." At the start-up, it was "overly formal" and "stilted."

But the biggest difference between this job and my previous ones was that this company was interested in making money. Frankly, I'd never before worked somewhere where this was a goal. At my last job, all my clients were poor criminals. Here, my clients were entrepreneurs who cared about the *bottom line*. I won't make you guess which clients I preferred. Which I more respected. And which I thought were smarter.

We had one client who gave very sassy feedback to our articles. This always made my editor angry and nervous. She would spin her wheels doing everything she could to avoid the harsh feedback. I never minded the feedback; it paled in comparison to things my legal supervisors had said to me. I just thought the client had a spicy personality. And I preferred her commentary to the passive aggression that was the norm at the start-up.

As with most jobs, I had trouble making myself care about this one. It was even harder than law. With law, I didn't believe in the system, but at least the goal was noble. I was advocating to protect the legal rights and secure the liberty of people who couldn't afford lawyers.

But here, the goal was—according to the website—to help founders gain exposure and build credibility through content creation. I have no idea what that means, but it doesn't sound particularly beneficial to society. One of my only work friends, who was fired in his first month, told me the company had a sound business strategy because it was, in his humble opinion, built on "taking advantage of idiots."

A part of me misses the law. The way writing briefs felt so satisfying and automatic, and occupied my mind. I got a high off telling the government it was wrong in precise, scathing sentences. But then I think about having another one of my briefs rejected or wearing a blazer under fluorescent lights or having to listen to another boring white man monologue about himself or my friend demanding I solve an issue with their landlord—and I'm relieved to know I'm no longer a licensed attorney.

The other day a friend sent me an op-ed she'd written in favor of a new California employment law. I wanted to read it and understand her points, and I knew I could, but I couldn't find the motivation to do it without a grade or a paycheck on the other end.

Sometimes my friends ask me for legal advice. When they do, my inner monologue is like: *I stopped paying my bar fees, I've never read a contract, I'm writing a book called* Bad Lawyer, *and I just walked into a wall from texting too hard . . . I am NOT your girl.*

A part of me thinks I'll never be fully satisfied or comfortable in this life. I keep thinking about the psychic toll of wanting things that society doesn't value, and not wanting things that it does—like reproducing, contributing to the economy, and starting a nuclear family. I often envied my entrepreneur clients because their lives were so mapped out and simple. They didn't seem crushed by the weight of their own thoughts. They didn't appear remotely ashamed about who they were or what they wanted, despite that their sad attempts at entrepreneurial success were low-key destroying the planet.

In *The Queer Art of Failure*, Jack Halberstam writes that there is "something powerful in being wrong, in losing, in failing."[3]

I didn't identify it as such at the time, but I admired Fernando's refusal to conform to society's rules. He didn't date or have kids, and he wasn't ashamed about either. He defended criminals for a living.

He wasn't PC or woke. He would wear sweatpants to work

and then change into a suit with his door open when he "had to talk to the boss."

He spent all his free time at the Jewish Community Center, despite being Catholic.

His behavior inspired me. Like, *it's my rules now.*

Law's main operating premise is: "It has been this way, so it shall remain this way." The law has a lot of reverence for the past, for convention, for predictability. But life isn't predictable. We're spinning in space! And no one knows why.

Life is arbitrary. There is no "reasonable man." People are mostly irrational.

And when it comes right down to it, we follow our own laws.

Acknowledgments

Thank you to my agent, Sarah Phair. Thanks to my editors Krishan Trotman and Carrie Napolitano, and the rest of the Hachette team.

Thank you to my early and insightful readers: Rachel Dempsey, Christie Bahna, Crissy Milazzo, KK Wootton, and Ana Reyes. Thanks to my writing group, Shitty First Drafts—Maggie, Robin, Catie, and Jon.

And thank you to my parents for not disowning me.

Endnotes

introduction

1   Niraj Chokshi, "Federal Judge Alex Kozinski Retires Abruptly After Sexual Harassment Allegations," *New York Times*, December 18, 2017, https://www.nytimes.com/2017/12/18/us/alex-kozinski -retires.html; Matt Zapotosky, "Prominent Appeals Court Judge Alex Kozinski Accused of Sexual Misconduct," *Washington Post*, December 8, 2017.

2   Jacob Anbinder (@JakeAnbinder), "the supreme court is best understood as a reactionary conservative institution," Twitter, June 27, 2018, 12:47 p.m. https://twitter.com/JakeAnbinder/status/10120599304661 11488.

chapter 1: the parents

1   Brian Hughes, "D.C.: The Lawyer Capital of the World," *Washington Examiner*, October 30, 2011, https://www.washingtonexaminer.com /dc-the-lawyer-capital-of-the-world#:~:text=An%20astounding%20on e%20in%202012,every%2025%20of%20its%20lawyers.

2   Michael Grass, "D.C. Has Nation's Highest Concentration of Lawyers,"

Huffington Post, October 31, 2011, https://www.huffpost.com/entry/dc-has-nations-highest-co_n_1067215.

3   Glassdoor.com, King & Spalding company reviews, January 15, 2015, https://www.glassdoor.com/Reviews/King-and-Spalding-Associate-Reviews-EI_IE3253.0,17_KO18,27.htm.

4   "Wet T-Shirt Lawyers," *Washington Post*, December 23, 1983, https://www.washingtonpost.com/archive/politics/1983/12/23/wet-t-shirt-lawyers/c46ac2e6-2827-49a7-9041-f00ac5f21753/.

chapter 2: the internship

1   Hamil R. Harris, "Locked Up with Roaches and Vermin: Activists Protest 'Inhumane' Conditions in D.C.'s Central Cell Block," *Washington City Paper*, July 31, 2018, https://www.washingtoncitypaper.com/news/city-desk/blog/21015773/activist-protest-inhumane-conditions-at-dcs-central-cell-block.

chapter 3: acceptance

1   Caleb Mason, "Jay-Z's *99 Problems*, Verse 2: A Close Reading with Fourth Amendment Guidance for Cops and Perps," *Saint Louis University School of Law* 56, no. 567 (2012).

chapter 4: law school

1   "As per a 2016 study more than 1 in 5 lawyers reported that they felt that their use of alcohol or other drugs was problematic at some point in their lives, and, of these, nearly 3 of 4 reported that their problematic use started after they joined law school" (Indra Cidambi, "Drug and Alcohol Abuse in the Legal Profession: Why Lawyers Are at Increased Risk for Addiction," *Psychology Today*, July 17, 2017, https://www.psychologytoday.com/us/blog/sure-recovery/201707/drug-and-alcohol-abuse-in-the-legal-profession).

chapter 7: death penalty clinic

1   "Race and the Death Penalty," ACLU, https://www.aclu.org/other /race-and-death-penalty.

2   David C. Baldus, George Woodworth, and Charles A. Pulaski Jr., *Equal Justice and the Death Penalty: A Legal and Empirical Analysis* (Boston: Northeastern University Press, 1990).

3   Baldus, Woodworth, and Pulaski, *Equal Justice and the Death Penalty*.

4   "1972: June 29: Supreme Court Strikes Down Death Penalty," History, February 9, 2010, https://www.history.com/this-day-in-history /supreme-court-strikes-down-death-penalty.

5   "Pennsylvania Death Penalty Costs Estimated at $350 Million," Death Penalty Information Center, December 17, 2014, https://deathpenal tyinfo.org/news/pennsylvania-death-penalty-costs-estimated-at-350 -million.

6   Graham daPonte, "Specializing," GrahamdaPonte.net (blog), June 24, 2012, http://www.grahamdaponte.net/specializing/.

chapter 8: kitty

1   Cindy Richards, "Fighting a Lie That Just Won't Die," *Chicago Tribune*, May 30, 1999.

2   Richards, "Fighting a Lie That Just Won't Die."

3   Richards, "Fighting a Lie That Just Won't Die."

4   Catharine A. MacKinnon, *Feminism Unmodified: Discourses on Life and Law* (Cambridge, MA: Harvard University Press, 1987).

5   Dinitia Smith, "Love Is Strange: The Crusading Feminist and the Re-pentant Womanizer," *New York*, March 22, 1993.

6   Smith, "Love Is Strange."

7   Andrew Hacker, "Standardized Tests Are a New Glass Ceiling: Women Do Better in Class and Worse on Tests—and There Are Conse-quences," *The Nation*, March 1, 2016, https://www.thenation.com /article/archive/standardized-tests-are-a-new-glass-ceiling/.

8 Rufi Thorpe, *The Knockout Queen* (New York: Alfred A. Knopf, 2020), 222.

chapter 9: not guilty by reason of insanity

1 "Boot Camp for UC Berkeley Law School Grad in Vegas Bird Beheading," CBSN Bay Area, October 16, 2014, https://sanfrancisco.cbslocal .com/2013/10/16/boot-camp-for-uc-berkeley-law-school-grad-in -vegas-bird-beheading/. (Justin Teixeira was convicted of a felony and sentenced to prison boot camp, and Eric Cuellar entered a plea to a reduced misdemeanor charge, was fined, and was sentenced to community service.)

2 Henry K. Lee, "Berkeley Law Grad Sorry for Vegas Bird Beheading," SFGate, May 13, 2014, https://www.sfgate.com/crime/article/Berkeley -law-grad-sorry-for-Vegas-bird-beheading-5472261.php.

3 *White v. Edley*, A141212 (Cal. Ct. App., Aug. 28, 2015).

4 Tyger Latham, "The Depressed Lawyer: Why Are So Many Lawyers So Unhappy?" *Psychology Today*, May 2, 2011, https://www.psychology today.com/us/blog/therapy-matters/201105/the-depressed-lawyer.

chapter 10: the bar

1 "Exam Rules," State Bar of California, https://www.calbar.ca.gov /Admissions/Examinations/Exam-Rules.

2 "Exam Rules," The State Bar of California, https://www.calbar.ca .gov/Admissions/Examinations/Exam-Rules.

3 "Mandatory Dress Code," Virginia Board of Bar Examiners, https:// barexam.virginia.gov/bar/barmdc.html.

chapter 11: clerkship

1 Amy Brittain, "A Sexual Assault Case Leads to a Devastating Allegation," *Washington Post*, October 3, 2020.

2 Jenny Holzer, *Abuse of Power Comes as No Surprise* (offset lithograph on

paper), Rosemary Furtak Collection, Walker Art Center Library, 1983, https://walkerart.org/collections/artworks/abuse-of-power -comes-as-no-surprise.

3   Roger N. Lancaster, "Sex Offenders: The Last Pariahs," *New York Times*, August 20, 2011, https://www.nytimes.com/2011/08/21 /opinion/sunday/sex-offenders-the-last-pariahs.html.

4   "What Is the Effect of a .23 Blood-Alcohol Level?" *Austin Daily Herald*, April 27, 2000, https://www.austindailyherald.com/2000/04/what-is -effect-of-23-blood-alcohol-level/.

chapter 12: escape plan

1   Elizabeth Wurtzel, "Elizabeth Wurtzel Confronts Her One-Night Stand of a Life," *New York*, January 6, 2013, https://www.thecut.com /2013/01/elizabeth-wurtzel-on-self-help.html.

chapter 14: bedroom lawyer

1   Susan Sontag, *As Consciousness Is Harnessed to Flesh: Journals and Notebooks, 1964–1980* (New York: Farrar, Straus and Giroux, 2012), 360.

2   Sarah Schulman, *Conflict Is Not Abuse* (Vancouver: Arsenal Pulp Press, 2016), 84.

3   Peter J. Coughlan, "In Defense of Unanimous Jury Verdicts: Mistrials, Communication, and Strategic Voting," 94, *American Political Science Review* 94, no. 2 (June 2000).

chapter 15: representing a rapist

1   "Sex Offenders Forced to Live Under Miami Bridge," *All Things Considered*, NPR, May 20, 2009, https://www.npr.org/templates/story /story.php?storyId=104150499.

2   Jennifer Wriggins, "Rape, Racism, and the Law," *Harvard Journal of Law and Gender* 6, no. 1 (1983).

3   Michelle Alexander, *The New Jim Crow: Mass Incarceration in the Age of Colorblindness* (New York: New Press, 2010).

4   Catharine A. MacKinnon, *Toward a Feminist Theory of the State* (Cambridge, MA: Harvard University Press, 1989), 124.

5   Chimamanda Ngozi Adichie, "We Should All Be Feminists," TED Talk, 29:28, November 2012, https://www.ted.com/talks/chimamanda_ngozi _adichie_we_should_all_be_feminists.

6   Elizabeth M. Schneider, "Feminism and the False Dichotomy of Victimization and Agency," *New York Law School Law Review* 387 (1993).

7   Tao Lin, *Taipei* (New York: Vintage Contemporaries, 2013), 26.

chapter 16: horny for the law

1   Rufi Thorpe, *The Knockout Queen* (New York: Alfred A. Knopf, 2020), 181.

2   Jonathan Van Meter, "The Awakening of Kim Kardashian West," *Vogue*, April 10, 2019, https://www.vogue.com/article/kim-kardashian-west -cover-may-2019.

3   Jack Halberstam, *The Queer Art of Failure* (Durham, NC: Duke University Press, 2011), 92.